GET RICH

BE THE VOICE

A fool-proof money management plan that delivers more choice for the things that really matter.

MEG

HOGAN

The information in this book and the links provided are for general information only and should not be taken as constituting professional advice from the book author.

The author is not a financial adviser. You should consider seeking independent legal, financial, taxation or other advice to check how the website information relates to your unique circumstances.

The author is not liable for any loss caused, whether due to negligence or otherwise arising from the use of, or reliance on, the informations provided directly or indirectly, by use of this book.

First Edition August 2017

Published by Digital Publishing Australia

ISBN - 978-1-64204-905-3

Dedication

'What is dedication: the willingness to give a lot of time and energy to something because it is important' – Google dictionary

My wholehearted core belief is to *fight for brighter futures*, animals and human species alike. To live is to be able to experience life to its fullest. No single creature on earth has any more or less right to be here. Being humane and kind is the backbone behind the fight.

"Self-education is key to bettering one's own life.
Influencing and leading by example raises one's
ability to be unstoppable."
~ Meg Hogan

Acknowledgements

My realisation is that there are so many people and situations that have lead me to be in a search to unravel the wealth train and find the greater me. I acknowledge you all. Without the ups and downs, the good and the bad, the exhilarating and the damn rotten moments, my drive to help benefit others would never have been achieved.

INSTANT ACCESS

Access your bonuses with the link below ....
also connect with Meg on Facebook

www.portfoliomasterymeghogan.com/book-bonuses

facebook.com/groups/brainstormingbusiness

CONTENTS

Introduction

Money … I just love how this word inspires me to want for more. Not a person wanting to be lavished in expensive material items but instead, reeling in the desire to win at a property deal. The want to help create a better life for myself and others. The desire to travel and learn the cultural unknowns. The family holiday that bonds our need of belonging. The music concert that radiates for days within. The food sensations that excite every sense. The seminar of a top speaker that shifts core beliefs and allows me to glow because of it. The list goes on.

My name is Megan and in Welsh it has the meaning of 'strong'. I am the second daughter of two. My father a miner/handyman and my mother, a hairdresser/housekeeper, kept a working household shared with plenty of pets. We grew up with a strong belief in family and were always pushed to be achievers. Today, I am a mother, an ex-wife, a partner, a business owner, a landlord, a developer, a consultant, animal protector and many more labels.

Being the author of this book and coach of Design Your Wealth Foundations program and The Winner's Mindset program, I help people get on track financially through education. From how to stretch out their income, strategies to grow the balance of their accounts, exposing wealth principles that can be applied in all facets of life, and to step forth with a killer mindset.

In their transformation, I see clients go from being change resistant to change aspiring. From thinking they have a lack of opportunities to now seeing and believing they have a wealth of opportunities. From being overworked and underpaid to (best of all) now being in control of their time and looking forward to being paid their worth. My belief is that this is all possible once we accept change into our lives and choose to get uncomfortable for the greater gains, and the greater gain for me is freedom of CHOICE.

My title GET RICH, BE THE VOICE is just that. The title not only means that you can find avenues to raise your wealth, so that you will have a better lifestyle and more security and control; and you also be armed with more opportunities and more choices in life.

The latter part of the title reflects my need to contribute which is a highly successful trait of the 'Rich'. Finding your obligation to serve another for a greater good. These are the occurrences in life that hit a chord and leave you wondering why something is happening in that way. You know when something just doesn't sit right with you and your beliefs... luckily, you now can be the voice that stands for wanting change.

If you can follow a plan that can help you take control of building wealth; then you can believe that it is possible to create change where it is needed. You can stand up for or fund something close to your heart, knowing that there is room in the plan for expenditure. Believe that it is possible to be the kind of person who can create change.

I've had some great successes in life. Starting out being a B-grade type of student, paying for self-education, being involved in loving relationships, having great kids and having a good resume of jobs in banks, energy and cash management companies. My passion was always centred around money, property and animal causes, where I had been fortunate to not only own our first house but also helped to build it. There is something really special when you put your heart and soul into a project. When it is completed, you look back and can get overwhelmed at what it meant to you. Since then, there has been many investment residential properties, a land subdivision, an established caravan park and a few profitable businesses thrown into the mix.

Struggle is what helps us realise what we are made of.

I remember how hard it was to get our first home loan, it took three tries and a lot of shifts in our daily routine to satisfy the bank requirements. This was at same the time as starting a young family while being reduced to one wage. Which was a casual labourer job that was not constant work. It is fair to say we struggled, no ... we barely existed to have a lifestyle.

Fast forward 10 years, we were getting tired of the night-shifts and day shifts of the jobs we had. Never really spending enough time with our friends or being around together as our family grew. Our focus changed. We were happy to earn a passive income from our rental properties, however, this got us really thinking when we were exposed to the lifestyle of a caravan park owner. Just think, many multiple comparable rents coming in with lower expenses than a house. Best of all, they seemed to have people staying there all year round. It was like we could be the mayor of a small village. We compared this to our trend of having rental homes and thought of all those weekly rents that could be collected during a year.

Then there was another drawcard that could be used later - the chance of selling out to a developer if in the right location, eyeing off the bigger land parcel usually close to a beach or water way that could turn into a townhouse development or the likes.

On a personal note, we knew it was time for us to be a close family unit again; we started getting excited over the little things like having the kids finally able to play club sports, how they could learn to drive the mowers, park vehicles and learn valuable life and business skills. We were convinced that buying a caravan park was the way to go.

In the search for a promising sea-change that would suit our new way of life, we marched into the local business brokers with all hope and excitement. Our new adventure could be about to start. We entered the meeting with a firm handshake and a cheerful smile. Out came the financial analysis papers to qualify us before he could tempt us with promising businesses he had in stock.

The meeting took a turn for the worst.

Only to be dashed when we were told we did not have enough equity to purchase a moderate coastal one million-dollar caravan park. We were shattered!

"No, that can't be", we were not ready to let that be the final decision. We had built our hopes and dreams for ourselves and our kids to have a complete life change and this broker said 'NO'. So, we just sat there. Probably quite stunned really.

He saw how much we wanted this.

After the initial shock, our meeting was revived. We started talking of options and possibilities. We felt like we were on a mission to find something that would leverage our equity into getting us the financial amounts required to get out dream to be realised. By asking the right questions and searching for the right team, we put it into practice. Luckily we eyed off a block of land close to the beach, esplanade shops and restaurants in the idyllic town of Hervey Bay in Queensland. Potential was there to subdivide the lots. It was just a fairly small land subdivision, but once sold, it would hit the required equity markers we needed. So we bought the block and engaged a team to help push the subdivision through. Sometimes, you have to take a risk and just go for it to reach what you really want. Several months later, all the blocks sold, and we were pleased to say we did make a lot of money in that short period of time.

The realisation one day as I sat on a child's swing, that not only had we succeeded the benchmarks of equity needed to change our lives, but we had gone beyond what was needed to get in the game. I was so proud of ourselves, and especially at myself grasping that next income ceiling at the tender age of 30, I felt we were and always had been lucky in life. The significance of that moment was upheld when we went back to the caravan park brokers - no longer were we ushered to the door, but instead out came the prospectus of the the $1.5 - $2 million dollar parks seeking our attention.

Gosh, if only I knew then what I have learnt in the lifetime lived; things may have been a lot different with the stakes being so much higher.

Eight years on, being owner-operators of a healthy caravan park business, stresses came to light. Life threw another curve ball that left destruction in its path. It was like being the eye of a tropical cyclone; that dreaded marriage breakdown. Showcasing those horrid emotions of fear, anger and deceit. Once we were a loving forward-focused couple, now we were not even able to communicate. No-one really predicted this outcome. We always thought we were lucky in life and we were soul mates. But when love disappears, your bestfriend title gets stripped away and you both walk around like you are a shell of your original selves. Change has to happen for your own survival. Please do not get me wrong, I would fight for family unity, strong bonds and a wonderful sense of belonging, but at the time, I felt I was the only one willing or capable of the fight. He too had to come to terms with his own ordeals and determine if there was anything left to grasp hold of in the name of family.

Divorce came.

Uncertainty arose, that two-income secure and modest lifestyle was then reduced to both starting again as single parents, shouldering our own massive financial loads to begin again. You could say I was a bit broken. Trying to find sense of what I really wanted, where I was heading, what new roles I had to play, who I was still friends with and who I wasn't.

But after a little while, I started to get a sense of excitement by new sensations, new foods, new experiences, new health kicks, new styles of clothes, new friends. I had found a freedom I hadn't experienced since I was 18 years old. It was time to pick myself up and fight back for the strong, happy person I was before. And fight back I did.

Finding my inner strength, regaining my power and pulling myself back together. I wanted to learn all I needed to know about how I could better my mistakes, get my financial position back and show my kids that you can rise from the depths as a better version of yourself. AND YOU KNOW, this is exactly what happened.

I had money from the divorce, our joint business had been sold, and only one asset was still shared. I had partnered in a start-up business. Our joint credit card was in my ex-husbands name and even though for twenty-odd years I had paid the bills, it did not help in my quest at having a credit history of my own. I had to prove to the banks that I was not a credit risk, again.

They posed ideas that to lend any money would require a modest deposit against a new house, tying up my funds for years ahead, so that it would halt my ability to gain traction in growing my wealth.

I had to learn to hold my ground advising I did not want to spend more than required of my money on my new primary residence purchase. But I also did not want to hear NO. DENIED LOAN. I had to think on this some more.

The bank was well within their rights to deny the loan as my new partner (yes, I did say new partner!) and I withdrew wages from the same source; our less than two-year-old start-up business. Both are big risk factors for a bank that alone are grounds for refusal.

I knew we would need persuasion and guts to find the right type of mortgage broker to be connected with a loan provider that could handle the risks of a start-up business. We all know that a loan needs 1 a security, 2 equity and 3 serviceability and although I had property with no mortgages attached, it was shared with my ex-husband and not of interest to any bank. I had equity in the form of liquid funds, of which they liked, but I was not willing to hand more than necessary over for a house mortgage. They did not like that we had a start-up business under two years old that we both drew a wage from for the serviceability criteria.

When I say it took guts and persuasion, it meant we had to find a broker that had already gone into bat for people who did not have bad credit ratings but did not fit the standard criteria and could present the application in a manner that would still have banks pitch an offer.

I needed the help of my team - my accountant and my solicitor. And thankfully, heaven and earth shifted, the loan was approved and the house was bought. A few third tier lenders came to our rescue, that once the appointed bank saw our financials and secure history of loans we were upgraded to a better and more comparable loan.

Following that year, after our personal residence was bought, we acquired two more investment rental properties and the asset I owned jointly with my ex was sold and upgraded to a few blocks of land for an upcoming development project and a retiring wealth account growing my future funds. Staying focused on my financial wealth and the path forward, within four years, I am happy to say I had once again acquired enough equity share to have my modest lifestyle revisited.

(Now it is time to do the dance!)

An important note to take away here is that there had to be a plan, a vision and an end goal. I was relentless in trying to get my financial status back. In the pursuit to feel whole again and more secure. My decisions at this time were based on how to utilise what I had in order to mould myself into what I needed to be to suit the criteria of the game. The game of money and building wealth.

We need to find the passion, the balance of lifestyle, work and the strategies to teach ourselves and our kids of the life we want to experience, that we can all live well within our own set of values. I was lucky and privileged to meet many wonderful, wise and successful mentors that could show me that we all have something to offer. We have all lived such intricate lives that no one else could match up to our own ideals.

Thus all knowledge obtained can be valuable and unique, but can also be helpful and shared by a broader common audience. My love of making change, making money and the good it can be used for, I pass on to you. As I write this in 2017, this is 6 years and over $100,000 investment in courses, programs and seminars, many hours learning the teachings, and I wish to share this learnt profound knowledge with you.

Chapter One

Get Out Of Your Head

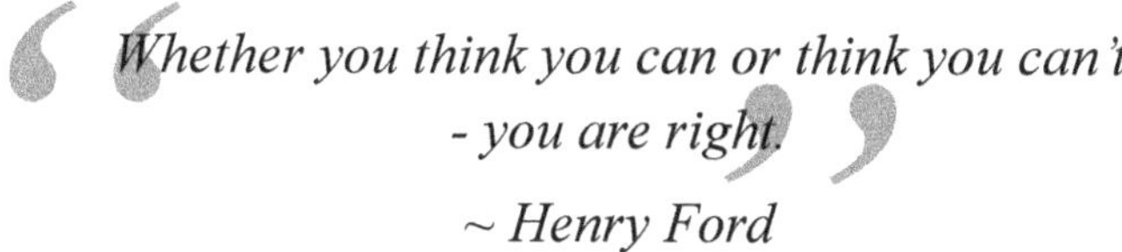

Whether you think you can or think you can't
- you are right.
~ Henry Ford

This opening chapter I want to focus on our mindset. This will be the incorporation of beliefs that we have lived by and the opinions we hold guarded.

Why you ask?

Too many times I have seen people locked into their daily habits, wanting difference, but unable to change for fear that if they do make a change, it could mean catastrophic circumstances for them and their 'comfortable' surroundings.

Well, I totally disagree… I love change. Let me repeat that – I

LOVE CHANGE! And you know why? I love change because it opens up new doors of opportunity. I am sent on another path of discovery that truly enriches my life after every change I make. I chose and still choose to be an Explorer and see life as a beautiful gift that all can share in.

As my ex-husband told me "Honey, one day you are going to have to learn how to change furniture and not the whole house each time". I must admit, he said this after about our twentieth house move. One may find that constantly updating the address book would be tedious to most. I was awakened to this fact when I was packing up my mother's house after she had passed away. Locating her little frayed cornered address book where there were pages and pages filled with people she knew. Not only addresses and phone numbers but other pieces of information like the weight of a new born baby, the names of the pets, etc. On reaching my name, I must have contributed to seven or eight pages with crossed out details and tiny doodling trivia that was occupied over the many years.

When I think about it, I have never been bored a day in my life. Changing jobs in my earlier years kept the 'I'm in a rut' feeling at bay. Being busy whisking here and there. Always itching to escape artificial lighting and cold air-conditioning of my office environments to getting back into the outdoors, smelling the fresh air, feeling the grass between my toes and loving being near water with the sun hitting my back.

But at certain points in my life, even though I entertained a lot of change, I still managed to get boxed in.

The sole reason I needed to modify the way I was, comes from comfortable thinking that felt limiting. Deep down inside I knew there was more to life than what I had known. Once I had accomplished a task, learnt the processes, simplified it as best I could to find an easier way, I found it tiresome to just keep doing the same year after year. It is not to say my life was bland, no bloody way, but it was that I had a yearning, an itch, something deep inside that I could never satisfy. I thought about it and came to the conclusion that I could do more, be more, travel, achieve and give more. I wanted the creativity back in my life, the freedom to laugh in hysterics, the money to create more choices and to feel the excitement as I ticked off my accomplishments and relished in the feeling of attainment.

So if you feel your want more, please join me, whole-heartedly, to disqualify any of your old limiting beliefs and negative doubtful self-talk. You and I are worth so much more and the ripple effect to others of the good we could do is endless. I want you to win for the sake of yourself and the sake of others.

Let's get uncomfortable and push the limits.

Life is there and let's claim our share.

So, who is with me?

•••

I have a friend who is very close to me. She is very smart, very talented, a born leader you would say. She has raised 3 beautiful children each aspiring to heights in the academic world, parading the titles of Duxes and Honoured Student, etc. She has devoted a lot of energy and beliefs so that these kids can push through and achieve anything they desire.

But what happened to my friend? She has a corporate job in low grade administration, she makes it her world. And her talents shine. But she is not rewarded, as the corporate system pays for time, for hours and time off in lieu.

You see the system has not rewarded her for the value she adds to their culture and vision. Instead it treats it and her as a 'time for money' job, and overtime has to be authorised by management for crucial projects.

Everybody can see she is worth so much more than the job she is in, but she has held onto a belief that this is the best she can get. Being a single mum she cannot afford change that might create an environment less than the one she exists in now.

She needs the certainty of security before she could ever risk change. She has dependents and a lifestyle that pushes the boundaries of her pay packet each week. Her limiting belief of fear that 'this is the best she could get', 'if she changed jobs, there might not be the consistency of work hours and her lifestyle might suffer', and 'there is lacking opportunities that could pay her worth'. So, she keeps doing what she is doing, settling, but makes it her goal to get better and better so one day someone in a higher role might take notice and promote her. I do hope that this strategy will work for her, but that was the way they did it back in the 1950's. These days, there are many people overly qualified itching to do what it takes to reach the few top spots and it can be a long road to a very worthy promotion.

Have you ever heard your inner voice screaming words of advice that causes you to doubt your intended step forth?

The common inner sabotaging statements I hear are:

"What if people think I am not so smart?"

"Work hard, get a good education and a good job then you'll make money"

"People are smarter than I am, why would they buy from me?"

"My mother/father would not approve"

"Being rich is criminal"

"Don't waste your hard-earned money"

"I can't sell to people"

"I cannot attract people"

"I cannot speak in public"

 "I didn't finish university, so what can I really offer"

"Am I good enough?"

Are you kidding? These and any more you think of are complete hogwash.

Let's get real – who or what are you comparing yourself to? Apples for apples? Is it just a feeling you are getting or been told from others (which probably was a joke at some point), why you would not be good enough? You are unique, no-one has lived your life the way that you have. There are people out there who will resonate with you because they understand you or have a sense of what you've done, they feel your vibration and are connected to you. Other people will resonate with differing kinds of people that are not like you, and they vibrate energy on a different frequency.

You must understand that when you were born you were 100% pure and whole. You were perfect. And then up to the age of 5 you were just a sponge , taking in views straight to your subconscious of everyone around you without question. Watching the behaviours of others, and learning how to be accepted in society. There had been rejections, humiliations, fear, and all feelings in between soaring and feeling enlightened. We have been moulded from people we trusted and opinions and thoughts that were passed down, feelings and stories were instilled in why we must behave like that and some stories may even have been just to prove a point, that were not actually about us at all.

When do you start to question what you have accepted as your belief?

Are they correct in what I have been told?

Do I actually believe it?

Why would those beliefs be correct?

Where has, that belief come from?

Was it even of our time?

Does it even make sense to me?

You'll find that most of your beliefs have never been challenged, we just blindly accepted them as the views were handed down by people we trusted, but guess what? … most of these beliefs have been the crap that held you back from thinking you could make massive changes in your life. You will find the moments that have stopped you, they will have an underlying feeling of anger or fear if you move too far from the boundaries that you set up to keep yourself comfortable and safe.

Think about this statement for a minute, this is big. Not only has your beliefs frozen you, when you should have soared in life, but they have also changed the lives of the ones surrounding you. Their comfort zones have been allowed to grow alike your own when you did not create a massive successful change for yourself. If you had, the people surrounding you would have watched and learnt how to take flight themselves for a greater life of purpose.

You also unknowingly hurt the people you could have served and raised up, helped or influenced personally. You see, you only have an undisclosed amount of time to make the changes you want in your life and show the next generation that all is possible, don't hold back, just go forth.

The ripple effect also stems out to the reasons you want to change now. It could have been a cause that you could have helped many years ago and now the recipients of help are no longer here existing with us. It could have been the money earnt that could have educated others for a greater cause. It could have been an invention that may have taken off, making the lives of others easier or more connected. It could have been a movement that pursued the government, a push where big business had to change their ways, mother-earth could have been helped by saying no to pollutants that would save our future generations. You get my point.

By having these negative self-talk moments and believing them, has slowed everyone down, including you and myself at times. Imagine the paths you could have been on, following your life's pursuits. Imagine the people you could have brought up to enjoy the wonder of life's pleasures if there were no self-judgements.

But you came back to the same realisation being that you only have this undisclosed amount of time to pursue your life. If you feel the need for change and can hold a vision greater than what you are living now. Take action and show others that you could be the ripple that sets a change in motion for not only yourself but all you come in contact with..

"I am the solution to someone else's problem",
"I am so happy and grateful to share in the abilities to help others",
"I am ready to expand",
"I am smart, confident and strong",
"I allow cash flow to enter my life in abundance".

How did you feel when you read these statements out loud? My guess is you felt confident and energised, uplifted. You should use strong statements and feel-good thoughts to feed your conscious mind. Your mind is amazing.

The conscious mind has the ability to accept or reject information given to it and the self-talk (good or negative) will protect this part of the brain. If it accepts information it is firmly planted into our subconscious mind. This part of the mind goes off and filters opportunities to fit this new accepted thought to bring about what you asked for. If the conscious mind rejected the new information, on the grounds that it may harm your survival, or it was not aligned with your belief system, then it would flush the notion.

The negative self-talk puts up an argument that if you accept this, your vibration would change out of its comfort zone. This is that "icky" feeling of self-doubt that can make you nauseated if you persist. Our body's way of protecting us from possible harm if we breach our comfort barriers.

The old adage of if you feed on enough positivity and feel good moments, there would not be room for any negative dwelling thoughts, you can only give out good positive vibrations I believe is so very true. Don't you think your negative self-talk would begin to fade as your belief system starts to change. Not only does your belief system change but your perspective changes too.

I mean, when having a negative belief in your mind, it changes your perception. If you thought you could not smile in photos and you were overweight, your negative belief system would adapt your thoughts to steer you away from being caught in situations that would make you slip into a lower depressed vibration.

It also warns you when looking in a mirror, it arouses bad "icky" feelings that distort how you look to qualify that belief, any photos you were in you would shirk at how dreadful you looked in that picture. But when you change to accept more positive thoughts and challenge that negative belief, you'll radiate a new positive feel good self-talk.

You'll find opportunities start finding ways to put you back in front of a camera, you'll be more visible in front of a mirror and you will not see what you focused on before. Your posture becomes more confident, yet you feel more relaxed, and a natural beauty is emitted. What changed? You saw a different radiated vibration. You raised your frequency.

There are infinite levels of frequencies. The universal source of energy is attracted to motion and high frequency vibrations. The attraction of a highly vibrating person is like the attracting poles of a magnet. You cannot help but come into contact with other radiating energy forces that are alike or forces that need more energy. Operating at a more heightened frequency, feels so much better than living with sabotaging beliefs.

Now there is a time to unload the burden and forgive…

If you have breezed through life without the need to forgive another, you have done well to this point. But for the rest of us, there will be circumstances that need attention. This can be difficult, but I know you want to move ahead and grow. It can make you have a sickening feeling when you cannot forgive a person for their actions. It has left a scar on your soul. How can you let that go? The anguish you feel can upset your digestive system, can rivet your confidence and rob you from your power. It also can make you very angry that all these states can dull our vibration and deflate our frequency. Plus our health in general cannot sustain long-term stresses without our cells erupting with disease. It again promotes negative self-talk and the cycle restarts, holding us frozen in our growth actions.

Sometimes, there cannot be forgiveness given. The incident too grave.

Think of it this way, you do not forgive the actions of that person but you do forgive the person, for they did not know the difference or the power behind their actions at the time. Now, is the time to just breathe in and out, feel that release and follow up with beautiful feel good visualisations. Forgive others from your past and let the feelings go. The only person still being hurt and halted is you. It is time to release it.

Change the focus…

This statement "Learn to be grateful" makes us operate from a very high frequency. It attracts and fills your body with feel good endorphins. It can change our state when we are stressed from fear or anger. It can restore our distorted perspective from being in a lowered state and allow us to see beauty and give feelings of how lucky we are to be a part of it. You cannot operate with a frown or grimace when being grateful.

There is plenty to be grateful for; our very existence, having people to love and who love us, being able to laugh, walk and express ourselves, giving inspiration to others, all of these things make life beautiful. You could be grateful for the teachings of a mentor, an understanding of a lesson, to having some time out to do what you want, etc. If practiced daily, being grateful, would change your vibration and people would notice your confidence soar.

We have all harboured toxic beliefs for too long, twisting up our guts, making our confidence slide. Well, what if I also told you that your memories or other people's memories may have been totally distorted and you've been hanging onto something that may not have happened quite the way you thought…

Remember, that depending on your beliefs – good or bad, your perspective on life will be affected. You can live in a real reality or a distorted reality... It has to do with the chemicals we produce to enhance the state we are in. Fear and negative self-talk will produce high levels of cortisol, which can have a shelf life of 24 hours. Whereas gratitude, conversation and positive affirmations will produce oxytocin, opening up your prefrontal cortex to a limitless amount of possibility.

Never assume where another person is and in what they see. Take a moment not to react, instead ask questions and try to see from their perspective what movie is playing in their mind. Offer up another perspective and see if you can find some common ground.

Could you see a good perspective, a bad perspective, which perspective would serve you and others better to make a win-win situation for all involved. Instead of reacting, ask your conscious mind to think and either accept or reject that information. Remember, we have the power to reject information if it does not serve us. People who offer advice or comments will understand that we chose to think if that information was right for us at that time.

Decisions should be made fairly quickly, do not procrastinate on a choice. You will have an instant feeling if there is doubt on a decision that could put us in harm. But if the decision will benefit your future's path, just commit to taking action. Making no decision at all is actually a choice in and of itself; a choice not change. Make a decision and if you feel uncomfortable with the actions or outcome tweak your path and push forward.

> *"The unknown path has more opportunities than the known prison of your comfort zone."*

So, with all this in mind, let's invent a new you.

We have heard people define us by our behaviour and situations we have landed in. Heck sometimes it was just because we reminded them of someone they knew, and we have even repeated this story as we have heard it so often by the people we trust and love.

But is it really true? Are you the Miss Scatterbrain that always needs the punch line explained in jokes? Are you the underachiever that will never amount to anything of good? Are you the college dropout that preferred to party and gave up any chance of having a successful career? Or whatever the condemning was.

Are we defined by this story?
I think we are **much more** and deep down so do you.
Does this story foretold by us and others help us soar ahead displaying degrees of confidence and no limitations or does it

put us in a box of self-sabotage and imprisonment? Anything that does not serve us should be screwed up and thrown away. Say "I" if you are with me here.

It is time to create the new you – draw from what you've done, who you've followed, who has inspired you, what has made you feel so high in life that it felt like you couldn't go wrong.

Find that shift that makes you feel strong, confident and elevated. Show off your emotions of when you were fun, kind and helpful. When you operate from a higher frequency, you attract those people to look at you differently. You are then open to another level of what you need at that vibration.

It is time to immerse yourself in people that are vibrating at a higher level, you need to keep evolving your story and believing in where you are going – following your dreams that are aligned with what values are important to you. This is your life. The only one we have and time is slipping away. There are no guarantees on how long we get to live our lives, so make the most of it. Start spreading your new story today and correcting the people who remember otherwise.

Take back your power and strive ahead.

Freeing up your internal mind space is so refreshing.

If you cannot fix it or change it, let it go.

There is no sense in beating yourself up any more. We are changing, we are growing and these incidents sculpted us, but do not and should not define us. Our story we tell and emit is just that, it is a story and it's focus on the negative is not needed any more. Learn to say YES, put yourselves out there more – hopefully in good circumstances. Watch the doors of opportunities open up, watch the on flow of situations occur that will excite your inner self. Guess what, you have a whole new story brewing of who you really are.

Chapter Two

What's Important To You?

*'And every day, the world will drag you by the hand,
yelling,*
*'This is important! That is important! And this is
important! You need to worry about this! And this! And
this!'*
*And each day, it's up to you to yank your hand back, put
it on your heart and say,*
'No. This is what's important.'

~ Iain Thomas

What are values? Scott Harris - Australia's Millionaire Mentor and Ultimate Coach Founder and his mentor Tony Robbins – just the all-time Guru of knowing people, defines human needs into six sectors, they are:

1. Certainty - Be safe with finances, cautious moves, having

enough to survive and knowing you'll have that tomorrow too.

2. Significance – different, unique, having notary.
3. Adventure/Variety – fun, risk, challenge, surprises, possibilities, differences
4. Connections - love and relationships, friendships, respect
5. Growth – not just survive, but be better, learn more, new opportunities, moving forward
6. Contributions – your time, money, skills, etc. are valuable, teach others, help others, stand up for what is important

It is said that we desire all of these but that at least two will be more dominant. We are all different people, from different environments and with different DNA. You know when you meet someone similar to you and it feels like you both just 'click'? On the other hand, a person who lives with Certainty as their highest value, might seem boring to a person that has Adventure as their highest value. To the Certainty person, the Adventurer could take too many unnecessary risks for their liking.

A Growth person who is on a quest for knowledge and self-improvement, may seem like they don't care enough to a Connections person, who would rather take time to nurture relationships. A Significance person who desires to be noticed and appreciated, would find a Contributor person helping others before themselves probably quite compatible, provided they featured in the experiences of the Contributor.

Whatever your order of values are, they must align realistically with who you want to be and deep down, who you really are. In saying this, a good solid relationship can still be had from the understanding of certain values that you wish to improve on in your own life and that the other person displays. If you have Certainty that is safe and comfortable, but you feel that you don't take enough risks, maybe you would enjoy more fun and adventure in your life. The partner you choose, may have that impulsive nature that loves to take spur of the moment weekends away or try something new, whilst also needing to have a deep-down grounding of certainty in their life to support this very nature. These two people would supply a bit of what each other desires and complement each other in their relationship. However, this is only true if both people are looking for the other displayed values. A relationship would not work well if one person just wanted Adventure without the need for Certainty holding them back.

Aligning your values with how you wish to live means continually striving to be a better person. There is comfort in knowing you are displaying behaviours in accordance with your values.

There is a strength and confidence that is projected when you are aligned. People can hear it in your voice and see it in your stance. You attract positivity. You also expect better values from others around you. You start standing up for what you believe in and stop being swayed by the masses. You create hope for those less fortunate and start to attract the right people into your life. You start to vibrate on a higher frequency and the Universe and its infinite source of power will take note. You will feel on top of the world, that suddenly everything is different and you feel passionate about life. You may notice how opportunities suddenly present themselves and that people want to be around you. There is an active light and pace about you. Your life just feels great!

Do you know that you cannot really help others when your true self is hiding? When you align your values, people will see something in you that is true and real and be attracted to that quality. People can pick up on an instinct that tells them when someone is not real, resulting in a lack of trust. When you show your true self it will resonate. Maybe they like what you stand for, what actions you have taken, or they identify with your beliefs. You just have to be true to yourself to have the greatest impact on those around you.

Ask yourself, "What changes do I need to make to achieve my

dreams and life goals?"

"What did I do to cause a particular problem, and what is needed to resolve it?"

"Am I having enough fun and adventure in my life?"

"Am I teaching the ones who look up to me good values?"

"Do I give appropriate time to things before retreating or quitting?"

"Are my goals realistic based on where I am right now?"

"Have I identified ways of further stretching my thinking?"

"Who can I match and mirror that inspires me to be a better person?"

As quoted by Alex Blackwell, The BridgeMaker Founder;

'The Dalai Lama advises "that you should open your arms to change but don't let go of your values". The values that resonate with him and that he wishes to pass down to future generations are: Appreciation, Belief in others, Caring, Commitment, Compassion, Cooperation, Courtesy, Dedication, Effort, Forgiveness, Friendship, Gratitude, Honesty, Hope, Integrity, Listening, Love,

Optimism, Patience, Respect, Right Choices, Sacrifice, Tolerance, Unity, Vision.'

So, I ask again, "What is important to you?" "What values would you want to live your life by and be happy to pass down to others?"

There are many circumstances that will present in life, good, bad and everything that resides in between. Before commenting or making a judgement, we should reserve our first thoughts and look for the wisdom and positivity within. Everything has beauty. Everything and everyone has special gifts. It is up to us to find them and appreciate them. The world will become a kinder and more compassionate place to live if we can erase negative gossip, judgement and criticism of others, before taking the time to understand them. One of mum's old sayings that I utilise in my core beliefs is: "If you don't have anything nice to say, just smile and don't say anything at all". On the other hand, if you feel that you could offer a helping hand to lift another person, then make contact. Help others in a grateful manner if they are accepting of your gesture.

We are now removing the idea that you are assessing whether someone speaks the truth or not, and instead looking for the positivity and wisdom that can come from it. For example, the argument may be that black is the new red. You may not agree with this in the true sense of the statement. However, you may agree that the suggestion might inspire people to be more outgoing and confident when they wear the colour black. Once the colour that represented death and mourning, today it can be utilised for a lady's sexy little black dress, or a nice sharp tuxedo. Remember, you just have to think in a different way about whether you accept or deny information that comes your way.

Setting targets or goals to reach is important so that you know you are achieving milestones. They also help you to see how far you have come and what you need to do to achieve the next one on your list.

Let's keep that end goal in mind when planning out your goals for each quarter or year. I find it always best to work backwards from where we want to be to where we are now. The steps will then become clearer on how to get from point A to point B. Why are goals so important? They are the measuring blocks to achieving another milestone and they provide the motivation to reach the next target.

Rewarding yourself when a goal has been reached is a really important factor. We all want not to have to make sacrifices without some reward or gain for our efforts. Our belief in why we want change must be ever present and spur us along when we hit moments of wanting to return to the comfort zone. Understand also that the comfort zone will <u>not be the same,</u> as we now have an awareness that there could be a better life for us. The voice of fear that sits in the background and wants to talk us out of uncomfortable situations, does so for pure survival reasons. It is not with the intention of creating a bigger and better reality for you and all that ripples off your existence. Just don't listen to that voice anymore.

Having small manageable goals, that are easily achievable in the short term, will keep this voice of fear under control. Keeping focussed and visualised on what the new comfort zone looks like will also quieten this inner saboteur.

Make sure you are journaling your achievements to look back on someday. You never know, they could also provide the strength and the push that another person needs to raise their existence to a new level.

But…

Every now and then, be aware that you will come across people that are critical of your every move for whatever reason. Maybe they will genuinely believe that it is not in your best interest to proceed. Do not allow this to deflate you and lower your vibration. Their reasons may be due to fear that you are changing, concerns that their own circumstances will be affected, or even that they will be left behind. It could be that you are challenging their belief system or that they see you now as competition. Whatever their reasons might be, their judgements do not serve any purpose where you are going.

Politely thank them for their opinion, but choose only to take it on board if it raises you up and opens your mind to new possibilities. If it does not, then discard it and let it go.

Only when you begin to shift in your mindset and actions will people start to respect your boundaries. Loved ones sometimes find it the hardest to accept why you want to change. They chose you and you chose them as a certain type of individual and you are now changing.

These changes can work like magnetic poles, either repelling or attracting in unity. It is important to understand what their desires are too and to work with both sets of values. This will allow you to raise each other up and to experience a better reality that involves both compromise and reward for each goal achieved. If there are some mindsets that do not wish for change, then it is advisable to limit the exposure that you have to any negativity. Always be respectful of the opinions of your loved ones, take them into consideration, but then move along. Seek the vibration of another positive person, whether in the flesh or via media, to restore your emitting frequency and energy levels. You have the ultimate power to accept or reject information, all you have to do is think positively.

The more we visualise the path to success, the more focused our subconscious will be. It is capable of sourcing opportunities and giving us ideas as we become more aware and stronger in our conviction. It cements a good belief in who we really are and what our new reality will consist of. Our subconscious mind cannot distinguish between reality and a false reality. When we are dreaming, we experience something that feels very real. However, when we wake, our conscious mind will advise us of what was actually real and what was imaginary. Visualising means that the opportunities that we have identified can be brought to our attention and it prompts us to take one step closer. It develops a sense of familiarity, thus creating a new comfort zone, one that has advanced forward from the old comfort zone.

Lesson learnt of what is important to you, is to think on it, journal it, keep visualising the newer you and where you want to be in every detail.

Chapter Three

Utilising The Universe

"If you are focused on problems, the law of attraction will bring problems to you faster than you can fix them. What you focus on expands."

~ Abraham

All my life I have know to watch for 'signs'. You know that gut instinct, that intuition you have, if only you stop for long enough to listen …

I had a deep down feeling that a sign would always pop up somewhere to let me know I was on the right track. Something that I just knew was meant for me alone to see. And without fail it does, time and time again. I did not realise that I had set the accepting beliefs in place and my mind had gone to work sourcing opportunities for me along the topic of what I was visualising. It would filter out unnecessary items of my reality to only make sure I notice things along the way that was in line with my path.

It is like you decide to have your first baby together with your partner although you have been to the park many times before, you were gob-smacked at how many pregnant woman were walking around, how many mothers and small babies were walking in front and behind you. It couldn't be that you had never noticed it before, but there are pregnant women everywhere. Why hadn't you seen it before, now it is like an epidemic! What just happened?

Your subconscious mind had been quietly filtering out what was unnecessary for you and allowing you to focus on other important things like relationships, your job, your inner circle, and so forth. When you asked for something different, your mind opened up more of the reality for you to see, low and behold there was all of this happening around you and it was undiscovered at the time.

I also know when to spring on a big decision when my whole body's energy ramps right up and I have such clear and acute processing going on. Generally, I don't sleep well for a few days as my body is on a high, my brain does not turn off thinking of the new possibilities ahead. You see, I think my whole body's energy gets so alive when I am following my own inner values, my core beliefs, my truth. On these occasions, I feel it, I know it, I simply JUMP!

You may be surprised by how much a dream board can become a reality without much trying on your part. When you place a picture or phrase/quote on a wall and walk past and note its existence many times a day, it evokes a feeling that resonates with you. Some would say it draws the source power from the Universe to help create that desire. It certainly is in your direct upfront focus. Many millionaires do not take this to chance, learning that many before them in history, depict the use of focus with universal source energy and understand that the source power is infinite and always present. Noting it needs to be felt, focused upon in great detail and asked for to advance their wealth and opportunities. Many enter into rituals that also help get themselves in a higher vibration to attract source energy more abundantly.

There is a saying that asks the difference between Millionaires and Billionaires, Millionaires focus on their goals every single day, but Billionaires focus and visualise their goals multiple times a day.

My friend Natalie Cook is one of Australia's famed Olympian

gold medalist 5 years over for volleyball. On speaking with her about this topic, she revealed that to help them visualise being a gold winner at the Olympic games, she needed to wear something of the colour gold daily, and to have rings that signified to them the rings of the Olympic symbols.

Visual anchors like pictures on the fridge of a holiday you want to take someday can help expedite the want to focus your attention in acquiring that desire. Have you also noticed that if you place a picture of a mentor on the fridge or on your phone wall paper, you will find that you try harder to succeed as their presence is before you?

The Law of Attraction is best explained by mentor and speaker Bob Proctor. He has made it his life's work in uncovering what this is really about. He explains that the world is full of energy, we are energy and all things in it. Energy travels at different speeds and vibrations sitting on an infinite number of frequency levels. When we are sad our vibration is very low and other people are not attracted to this. When we are excited, our momentum picks up, we are buzzing and other people like to be around us. It is true that the energy can be taken by others or you can feel better by being around another person if you are lower than they are.

If you have ever been in the company of a negative person when you were feeling full of energy, you will notice that one of two things happen. You will either pick up on their negative energy and start to feel low, or they will pick up on your energy and feel better. When two energies that are the same high level are in a room together, the vibrations and positive feelings are multiplied. The idea that the different states we experience (i.e. happy, positive, angry, moody, in gratitude, etc.) changes the amount of vibration we emit.

It is depicted that this Universal source energy is infinite. People over many generations have witnessed changes in influencers when tapping into this source energy. Bob Proctor preaches from a book by Napoleon Hill 'Think and Grow Rich', written in 1937, where he was asked by the richest man at that time Andrew Carnegie to interview many great important men to understand how they became rich and understand if there was a common theme. What mindset they were required to have in doing so?

What Hill discovered was this …

The many well-to-do people he interviewed all shared a common trait of visualising They needed to understand with great clarity and depth what they wanted.

Some inherited their wealth, others made their own wealth. They just had to have a vehicle for making money and the need for many people to want what they had. They had to have a plan, spend less than they made, invest in themselves, use other people's time and money, and a desire to keep pushing for bigger opportunities.

To ask the Universal source energy for something was like praying to a god. They had to hold such a good flow feeling, be in a high vibrational state and ask with such clarity. Some say it is just your subconscious locating opportunities for you. Others would say it is so much more. They say the power it has can only be explained by how big your belief is in your focus. Everything is possible if your belief is big enough.

Bob Proctor has taken time to recognise that through another person's experience, the Universal energy is controlled by laws, like the many explainable laws we have displayed in our sciences (i.e. Law of Gravity – what goes up must come down).

There is a Law of Compensation – explaining that the amount of money you will always earn will be in direct ratio to the need for what you do, your ability to do it and the difficulty in replacing you.

And the Law of Attraction is based on your belief, your vibration and the desire to want it for the balanced reasons of the good it can do for you and others. However, this is not a quick fix for getting everything you desire. The laws will work only with a pure focused belief. A belief not ridiculed by blocks or negative belief patterns. This belief has an active momentum of doing good, and is immersed with good vibrations.

If the desire has not been thought out well enough in a clear understood fashion, another similar gift may be presented.

I had a very similar situation in early 2016, where I thought about wanting a white SUV (car), that was automatic and reliable. It had to have room in the back for the dogs when going to the beach. A few months later, a tragedy happened, my mother's fight from cancer was too great and she passed. Her white SUV was unexpectedly offered to family members but in the end it was left to me. I did not see it at first as my manifestation. It was not quite as I imagined. But I did notice that it had all that I asked the universe for. I sat quietly, thinking of Mum and then just laughed. It seemed, I had overlooked a very important lesson - I was not clear on what I wanted. But my Mum had her presence all over it. It was not a newer model, but rather a 2002 model Subaru Forester, bit boxy in look and a tad dated, but enough room for the dogs in the back. A good reliable little car with great fuel economy. A peace came over me. I dabbled in a practice and yes there is powers that work but only for what you can ask for with such clarity and certainty and are ready to receive.

There is a level of vibration like a music note on a bar. Except there is an infinite number of frequency bars that can be attained. The states we are in all have different vibration levels mixed with the level of vibration the person is already in. No two people are exact, but can be on similar wavelengths. You can feel this when another person is just so comfortable with you, that you both get excited, charging each other's vibrations at the same time. It is the same when two frequencies are too far apart, it feels awkward, and like a magnet that has been turned around, both deplete their own vibrations. The survival instincts kick in to try and move you both away from each other. Then there are moments when other vibrating persons can give (uplift another person) or take vibrations (depletes their energy) and the attract or detract instinct kicks in.

When you are on top of the world, there can be nothing that can bring you down. The sun is shining, the temperature is wonderful on your skin, your hair and body glow, people can see this and want to radiate towards you. You find things are easy to do, they take no time at all, your spirit sings within, and genuinely, things you want just fall into place. You could say your attractiveness was high on this day. On the other end of the scale, when things are not going well and you are on a low vibration, things seem hard, it takes so long to get anything done, people are at you, you just want to turn off the world and hide. Your attractiveness was present but attracting the negative surrounding us. All ill-feelings like to send us back to our comfort zone for shelter and security.

Remaining on the higher frequencies via working on being more positive, forgiving, being grateful and spiritual you can begin to raise your vibrations. Repetition is key to keep the energy active. Universal energy works best when you are on a higher frequency and full of active momentum for good for yourself and others.

Take a moment to really visualise and feel your ideal future reality.

"What date is it?"

"What colours are present?"

"Who else is there with you?"

"What temperature is it?"

"Is it loud or peaceful?"

"Is there water nearby?"

"Can you see a future happening there?"

"What is it?"

"What good for others are you involved in?"

The amount of depth and clarity you can get to in your vision when activating the Universal source energy, will see greater realisations of the manifestation.

Some would even take it bit further and enacting some pressure on the situation. Sandy Gallagher of the Proctor Gallagher Institute, wanted to purchase a house that was outside her earning capacity at the time. She went to the open house, special invite only and the house was beautiful. She sat in each room envisaging what furniture was there, who was living in it, what the smells from the kitchen wafting through each room was, etc. She really became one with all the rooms. The time came and Sandy thought, it would be lovely but I couldn't really afford it. Her confidant and partner in business; Bob Proctor was going to teach her about believing she could harness this power. He made her put an offer on the house, even though it was more than she could afford at the time and then pushed her belief more to proceed to send out Christmas invites to all her family members advising that Christmas festivities would be held at her new address – the address of this house that she had not acquired yet. Sandy was beside herself with worry over this decision. But the more she believed in herself and the vision of what could be and not giving into the fear of humiliation from family and friends of a possible Christmas prank, miraculous things started to shift, her offer was accepted and her earnings increased to cater to the new repayments. And you know what?

… She did have that Christmas party in her new home.

You will hear the saying 'Say YES and the how will be presented'. In this instance that transpired. She had a vehicle that had no cap on earnings being a partner in an educational business, and her personal stake in the company allowed her to accept more money inwards from higher trading. She realised that all she had to sell a few dozen more courses per year to create enough money to cover the new repayment. She had a clear focus of creating a new life in this house and a vehicle that could expand, a need to make her dream become a reality.

You will by now acknowledge, that what you project into the Universe, does eventually deliver something like what you asked for or were focused on if you were open to receiving. Beware, it may not be as you quite expected. But to dream of a better destiny and to be active in engaging goals and opportunities to stay on that path, will evoke a totally different Universal response. It is up to you whether you want to 'better' yourself and others.

Your reticular activating response will see to that. I know of a lady who simply applies this to her daily life – even when she drives to a carpark in a busy shopping mall. She envisages that she has just parked the car in a rock star type carpark (you know, the one that is undercover, not far to walk, and is not tight to get into). She mentally pictures this before she goes and has a self-belief that she is really lucky. And guess what happens most of the time… (maybe she is just lucky… maybe there is more to this than meets the eye).

Chapter Four

What Can You Do Today That Can Improve All Your Tomorrows?

> 'There are those who make things happen, there are those who watch things happen and there are those who say 'what happened?'
>
> ~ Robert Kiyosaki

With this topic, we are going to get into a habit of rewriting your goals and future path daily, taking time to immerse yourself in the feelings it gives, visualising the surrounds, smelling the aromas.

Journaling not only will get information out of our minds that rattle inside, but also add clarity to what should be achieved in that day or week, what feelings we had and whether it is a priority task or not. Twenty minutes of quiet time to plan, focus and discover the inner workings is a crucial part to creating a mindset change. There are certain people that can just make a decision, right or wrong and just decide to go with it and seem to land on their feet every time. There are other people that must investigate and compare before making a decision. Only when they know in their heart it was the right decision, they go for it. There are some people that never make a grand decision as they fear they might choose poorly.

I am here to tell you that it does not matter. To make a decision light heartedly or well discovered is still creating action and momentum. Opportunities present themselves via momentum and change. If you avoid decisions, you will never experience the gift of doors opening and the surprises that lay behind them.

In knowing this, it has always been a successful trait to make decisions quickly as not to lose the vibration or desire. Believing that the 'how' will present itself when you are ready. But if you have to change your decision, please do it slowly. Remember, those open doors of change may not have all closed yet and some change actions have already occurred. Reversing a decision can be sending you back to the comfort zone. No change occurs, no doors of opportunity, no heightened vibrations of excitement or surprise or achievement will occur - until you make another decision to just go for it. When it feels right and you're extremely excited, you can't sleep properly as you mind is working overtime. It is a good thing. Obviously, your mind has determined that it is working congruently with your values and it is trying to show you a sign that it is excited.

Simply understanding that money matters and life becomes more interesting with more money opportunities. To not have enough funds, denies you opportunities and a greater lifestyle. I enjoy that more money allows me to give to causes that can do so much for others.

On a personal note some of the causes I am passionate about are: Animals Australia - a cause that is dear to my heart. I have watched the suffering and tremendous fear an animal goes through before being slaughtered for our consumption. I have watched the hens that could never stretch their wings and dust around in the dry soils, the pigs that never felt sun on their backs or the frolic in the muddy waters of the meadow, the offspring of dairy cows that could not be shown love by their mothers or were not allowed to grow old. So much horror we commit to these calm beings in the name of food production. I hate that animals are not given the fair go to enjoy their very short lives and do what comes naturally.

Another cause is Soi Dog in Thailand. This charity hospital rescues domestic dogs and cats off the streets and gives medical attention to their homeless scars and wounds. They are immunised, de-sexed and microchipped then returned to their found locations. Without them, many animals would not have much of a chance living off the streets. They fight the fight to stop the cruel and barbaric dog meat trade, which is very prominent in the northern regions near the borders. Being a devoted animal lover, these types of organisations are my choice to offer help.

The way in which I can help others is through education, lifting the knowledge of readers and helping apply wealth strategies that in turn raise their financial standings and worth, in the hopes that all participants can look for causes that need their stamp of change and can actively create a better world for future generations.

The programs I offer are firstly on mindset and how important it is to get the winning attitude. The next program is about setting up a money management plan that can pretty much run in the background of life and build on your wealth each day. It is about having a plan to reach retirement without fear of not having enough.

Then, delving deeper, I uncover the principles of wealth creation. General rules that should be applied when wanting maximum gains to grow your money.

Wealth creation is such an interesting field and it can affect everyone. The principles have been depicted for many generations and refined as our generations evolve but our economies, trends and personal greed changes our priorities when to use these principles.

Finance is not taught enough in schools - don't you think that is strange? We all use money, we all judge ourselves and others by the status gained through wealth during the years. Shouldn't we all know how to control money wisely and build wealth?

Luckily for me, there are many people out there that do want to know more on how to improve their situation. Looking for the edge to nudge ahead in their own wealth building projects. The problem is it is not as easy as just following principles that have been laid out. Life gets messy and changes the ballgame. It is more about juggling the circumstances that box you in until you learn how to manoeuvre around them and plan a few moves ahead. It is about following your truth. That is not the same as another person's journey. And how comfortable with being uncomfortable trying to win at the game of mastering money and risk. But we all know that time is our greatest commodity. It just keeps counting down to an unknown date in the future and we lose time when we don't take action.

This chapter sets up a money plan that anyone can choose to follow. It allows for growth, play or risk spending, contributions and holidays. You hold control and can decide how other money opportunities can interact within your world. Changing your perspective and allowing other strategies to broaden your belief systems and what is possible, in turn spurs creativity to flow through realising that your existence can be more rewarding than you ever thought possible.

I learned some of these principles early in life, understanding the value of money and how you don't just spend greatly on items that do not hold their value. But watching my kids today making their life decisions about money has made me want to educate them more than what I needed to get by. You see, the value that the items purchased in my day (and I am not that old, just time has evolved more quickly) have changed. A house could be equal to 5 x your yearly wage to purchase, now can be 12+ years of uncertain wages for the same. The time for financial education is now. The timelines to achieve wealth is minimising when you apply the same value ideals to most things we want in life. But learning to manage money; understanding how to grow money and focus on your path of what you want and where you are going, and utilising the resources of today's world, changes the game plan.

Yes, it is the time to sit up and take notice. We need to start by measuring where we are at right now and where we are going to. For most people, this section of measuring is not sexy, but needs to be done, and done regularly. If this is not of your personality type, see if your partner gets more excited over this part and is willing to keep track. If not, you may have to tell yourself a story that helps you get in a position that you need to know this data – and yes, all good entrepreneurs know their numbers, whether they sourced it themselves or hired people to do it. It is the key ingredient to know where the next marketing dollars should be spent wisely, when the next bank loan can be sorted to snap up an undervalued deal, or when you've just hit a milestone and you can feel fabulous because of your achievements.

In this section, we are going to find out where and how much money is coming in. If any is passive income, or just active income. What expenses occur regularly and what are the impulsive expenses? What loans are crushing us and what are we taking care of? What equity are we growing each month/quarter?

Now let's cover some financial terms ...

What is *earned income*? Any form of money received (can be post tax) as a job or drawings (pre tax) from owning a business.

What is *passive income*? Any form of money received (can be pre-taxed or post taxed) that is derived by you not actively working for it (trading time/products for money). This can be positively geared rental income, online business or product sales that others operate.

What is *portfolio income*? This is income similar to passive income but from paper investments, like share dividends, interest on bank accounts, bonus/gift amounts, etc.

We all understand that *expenses* are our daily cost of living whether needed or wanted.

The n*et monthly cash flow* is determined by identifying our total income less our total expenses.

Assets are liquid money in the bank, stocks and bonds values, mortgage offset account balances, superannuation balances, property values, business values, items that have the ability to go up in value over time.

Nonsense Spending is anything like contents, cars, jet ski's, or toys that you spend money on and would class it as an asset for value, but if you had to resell these items, they would lose value.

Liabilities are different to expenses as they have an expiration (with a contract). Things like loans or credit cards, store cards, education debts, etc.

Net worth is derived from the Assets totals less the liabilities totals.

How long could I survive on my cashflow and net worth amounts is always an interesting figure. Some will have a sense of unease knowing how vulnerable they are right now and others will have a sense of ease as they have some time up their sleeves to turn around a situation if that need arises.

My free Monthly Financial Tracker spreadsheet is given as part of my website introducing my programs

1. Design Your Wealth Foundations and
2. The Winner's Mindset

Great tips and resources can be found there.

Grab your free Monthly Financial Tracker spreadsheet from this link: **www.portfoliomasterymeghogan.com/book-bonuses**

Otherwise, you can just arrange the data on a spreadsheet to see where the health is of your finances.

After the first time in compiling this information, the time taken can be greatly lessened, especially with today's apps that can find data on your phone faster than rifling through tax boxes of paperwork of years yonder.

This report will be the main point of discussion at a brunch date with your partner. Remember, if you have a partner, it is so important that you both move together in your decisions about money. If you are single, an accountability partner is preferred to help spur each other on to growing each one's respected wealth.

Now just to remind people reading this, legally I am obliged to tell you I am not a financial adviser that is selling you other companies products. My plans and principles of wealth creating is my deciphering of all the paid for information I have taken on board from many mentors over the years. I have thought how best to formulate the gathered data and I am proud to offer my abridged plan. I do not take into account your financial history or capabilities when disclosing this to you. The reader is under no obligation to accept my work as their truth but can relate it to their situation as they wish. Further to this statement, I am proud of this plan and hope you find some insight that may inspire a brighter future for you.

1. ***Schedule Sunday Brunch Monthly Financial meetings*** with your spouse/partner or an accountability partner – to discuss balances of where each account is, next month's goals, is it on track for your yearly goals? Make sure you have filled in the Monthly tracker. These meetings can be extended to quarterly once the habits have been formed

2. ***Set up your bucket accounts;*** let's work on one wage of $750 per week, I know this is a low figure but I want to show you that even a weekly wage like this can still build wealth via a plan. Please adjust to your family take home nett

wages. We are going to adhere to the Pay Yourself First rule of getting wealthy. The accounts should be fee free and interest bearing like virtual accounts

Trading account

Income account to handle income and expenses, including loan repayments – 60% ($450/$750, $23400pa). Your mix may be different to mine, but you need to make it work within your means. Food $80 (11%) Car & Petrol $30 (4%) Rent / Loan payment $135 (18%) Electricity & Utilities $15 (2%) Leisure/ Save $50 (6%) Credit card $80 (11%) – donate, bills, impulse buys **Salary Sacrifice $60 (5.5%) – already deducted before you receive nett pay.

TC Savings Account

20% ($150/$750 - $7800pa) – Other incomes received - Investment property income, nest egg funds, deposits, bulk expenses – only on major expenses that have to be paid. This account will handle the debt repayments, the deposit for a house, the extra loan repayments and the future wealth top up payments.

TC Investment Account

This is your risk account – 10% ($75/$750 - $3900pa) - splurge on tax lotto's, clothing, doodads, casino, shares, what-ever you wish to splurge on that has an upside to recoup funds. If you purchase doodads, you are purchasing items that you can resell later hopefully at a profit. Any winnings get invested back in this account.

TC Holiday Account

10% ($75/$750 - $3900pa) - this can be for holidays, weddings, education, etc. – the bigger long-term expenses.

Termed Account

Initial $2000, compound interest (cannot touch as crucial to retirement wealth).

Wealth Growth Fund Account (Super Fund)

Salary sacrifice 5.5% your wages contribute to Super Fund (deducted from your wage $60/$750 - $3120pa). Your employer or business should be paying the state standard super guarantee (presently in Australia 2017 is 9.5%). We are going to use the power of compound interest here over time to build funds exponentially.

3. ***Rid your debts*** (except home loan & HECS) – prioritise costlier first. Rid car loans, credit cards with smallest balance first, only consolidate if via a bank or credit

union, credit files will tidy themselves over time, do not go bankrupt unless guided by Financial Counselling Australia (not for profit financial counsellors) or similar to your country. Utilise your normal Trading Account for the maximum you can pay in salary sacrificing and top up with funds from the TC Savings account.

- *Renegotiate a lesser fee of interest* and no annual fee on credit cards with debt.

- *Use the amount that paid out a card and use it against the next debt* with its minimum repayment, until it has been all paid out… and so forth, ie, the first credit card had $25 minimum repayment + our $150 (20%) from the TC Savings account – once paid off, then the next credit card has $45 minimum repayment + $25 minimum of the first credit card that is no longer active + $150 (20%) from the TC Savings account, and so forth for each debt.

- When paid out credit card debts, *only utilise a Visa Debit card* on your Trading account. Later, once the debts are clear, then you can utilise a low limit credit card.

    4. **Double your Income** – add a side freelance gig, ask for overtime, climb the ladder, write down your financial

goals and focus on them each day.

5. ***Buy your home*** (PPR – Principal Place of Residence) – after paying down your debts with the TC Savings account, we then can save the 20% deposit with this account. Save like crazy! Sell items if necessary to raise deposit funds. Extra funds can come from the double your income exercise.

- *Look around for the best deal* and a good interest rate, within your price limit of repayments that also would cover rates, water and insurance.

- Utilise an offset account to pay into that covers your rates and insurance which will accumulate and reduce the interest until time to pay repayments and bills.

6. ***Wealth Growth Fund Account (Super)*** - wealth accelerate your future – Business collectives are good stock to rely on as business holds up the economy and the tax law is designed around it to keep it prospering. An employer account is suffice or a minimum balance of $500-$2000 to open a private account with the Indexed Balanced Funds = choose the cheapest online managed funds and choice to choose your own type of shares where you can be paid

dividends re invested back in the fund. Hold for the long term. Set and forget.

- Super Guarantee is 9.5% gross wages, up that to 15% by salary sacrificing – contact your super fund to advise this is post tax funds. Aim is to have enough funds in retirement that can cope with yearly rising inflation.

7. ***Multiply your Termed Account*** – top up this account with whatever you put in your TC Savings Account 20% accounts for 6 months.

8. ***Rid the PPR loan,*** save money – Regularly renegotiate a lower interest rate, try not to fix a loan as there could be inbuilt fees that are not in a variable loan, make extra repayments via the 20% TC Savings Account, live within your means.

- TC Savings account 20% was used for financial hiccups, then ridding your debts, building a deposit for PPR, topping up your Termed account for 6 months, now for the *extra mortgage repayments.*

9. ***Retirement Goals*** – paid off home and $250,000 in super

and as of 2017 in Australia, Centrelink can top up to these figures, if you have more, you don't need Centrelink. Never retire, just keep earning something on the side. Based on couple: Aged pension $34,252 + Super pension on $250k is $12,500 (5%) + $20,000 work = $66,752pa.

- At retirement, you are moving the balance of your Termed account to your Super account where you will should not pay tax on the interest earnt. The laws can change so entrust your advice from your accountant. Invest the Termed Account balance into a cash sector as a safe option and redirect all dividends to the Termed account to supplement your retirement wage.

10. ***Leave a legacy*** – put all important documents together – advisors, bank accounts, investments, insurance policies, funeral instructions, personal documents, entity information, passwords, up-to-date will, video of your parents and family history, letters to your beneficiaries. This can be done at major stages in life and continually being renewed as new information arises.

- *Donate to a cause or create your own fund for a cause,* volunteer your time and some of your money to help non-profit organisations change the ways of the planet that your believe in. Put your focus on what is important and what can be achieved by contributing. TC Investing or Trading account can handles the donations.

Now that is a basic money management plan to make sure you don't have to stress too much about your retirement.

Next, we understand what these categories of Income, Expenses, Assets and Liabilities are, but how do we manage money within them? To be clear, working from the end goal to the present, we ultimately wish to see our income going to support asset growth that deliver a return (cash flow) and can pay down our liabilities and expenses.

Let's say that again…

"Ultimately, we wish to see our income going to support asset growth that deliver a return (cash flow) and can pay down our liabilities and expenses."

At different stages of life, we have a different flow occurring. See which one you can relate to now:

Families A will often be seen as income going to expenses, no assets and a larger liability debt. Without assets, the reliability being completely on income and extending the liabilities makes it difficult to get out of this flow.

Families B will often have a scenario being good income of earnt, passive and or portfolio, a retrospective amount of expenses to what has been earned, assets that are still covered by high liabilities.

Families C will have income derived from cash flow assets mainly passive and portfolio well diversified to handle the risks, paid off liabilities except for the newly acquired assets, expenses which would be minimal as they would be written off as a percent basis in a business structure. The ability of the assets column to grow in value over time also enhances the income derived from assets each year.

Naturally, we would like to be financially comfortable and Families C flow of money would be our ultimate goal.

Transforming to a Families C money flow would need us to rid the debts that hold us back. But it is a good thing to know whether the debt is a Good Debt or a Bad Debt.

Let's start with Bad Debt – this is debt that the asset obtained is depreciating in value or it was for a good time and it was a debt incurred for an experience. The only exception to changing whether this becomes a good debt or a bad debt is whether you required this thing to create cash flow (i.e. a vehicle for courier driving, a holiday for a live event that sold other products, a photo shoot that was sold to a magazine, etc.). Buying a house is not a bad debt as it can create cash flow and it can appreciate in value over time, but buying a jetski for weekend use is, as it deflates in value and does not add to your overall income.

Good Debt is a debt that will increase your earnings, add cash flow, purchasing more appreciating assets, etc. Like educating yourself in a skill you will use in your work life is a good debt as it will potentially increase your earnings, purchasing a friendship ring of $2000 would not be considered a good debt as the ring would generally not appreciate in value.

The idea is to get liabilities (loan contracts) on good debt and utilise asset returns on bad debt items as you desire them. Let me explain, if you really wanted that jet ski (a bad debt) and could give a hundred reasons why it would make your life so much more fun, then you would need to find another asset deal that has a routine positive cash flow amount (after costs = cash flow positive income) to the same amount or higher of the repayments of the bad debt contract. Utilising other people's money where possible and reduce your risk as not to utilise the base funds of your assets or wealth accounts. Your out of pocket expenses for a $4800 jet ski is approximately $220 per month over two years. Very doable to find an investment where you could either refinance the difference within your pre-existing asset or acquire a new asset where in both cases, the asset creates a stable cash flow to cover the amount. I would suggest increasing the amount required to cover any emerging costs not factored in.

"But it is only $4800, can't I just pay it off from money in my account?"

You could, but the idea that one $500 a month payment missed on a wealth building compounding interest account can reduce your retirement balance by $16,000*, and this is just one month payment missed. If you did utilise the $4800 from the wealth account early on, it could cost you around $153,000 in retirement funds. Imagine if you utilised this account to take care of bad debts and the balance kept reducing. Not a smart move.

*This is based on the average 7% interest over a period of 50 years.

By finding money in a positive cashflow investment it does not harm your bottom line that is growing your future.

Bad debts should be paid off firstly in place of good debts. Bad debts generally will not be used in tax deductions (some will) and the interest rates when activated will be higher than a good debt. I would list all the debts in order of percentage rates, amounts and whether good or bad debts. I would pay the 20% amount from the TC Savings account on top of the repayment required. And the minimum repayment off any further debts. This is utilising the same concept of compound interest that reduces the balance quickly. And once that debt has been paid off, don't stop paying that minimum amount, add it to the next debt. In other words, focus the same repayment on the next debt with the minimum repayment and the TC Savings 20% on top. You can see that although you just keep paying the same amount over all the debts, as the debts reduce, the amount of the remaining debts increase. Genius way to squash debt quickly.

Higher education government loans should take care of themselves, in Australia when you make over $53,000 any refund amounts you deserve after a tax assessment will be forwarded to this loan. If you die before it is paid off, the loan insurance will take care of any outstanding debt and it stops there (your children will not have to look after this debt). But remember, government laws are always subject to change and your Accountant will have more timely advice on this subject.

The house loans can be paid down after all debts are paid out and you have topped up your termed account. However, if you buy and sell properties a few times and manage to create a surplus, please do eliminate other property debts and understand that you may need to place some funds into the offset account as there may be a capital gains bill on properties (in Australia) other than your PPR (principal place of residence) or small amounts on your PPR if you rented it out for a defined term whilst you were away. Remember, your Accountant will have the latest information on this matter that you should seek.

An under-used strategy we should do when starting out is to fall in love with Compound Interest. It is a beautiful thing when there is time on your side. All kids should be taught this straight off in life and everyone's retirement could be taken care of. The more you put in a fund at the beginning and then let the interest just get rolled over back into the investment year after year can be massive compared to the initial amount you actually invest over time. If you did the same scenario later in life with half the gestation time, your investment would be almost halved. Time to compound over and over with the interest added produces exponential growth of funds. By adding to the investment say $100 per month early on would also see great benefits to the account holder than to add these funds at the later part of the investment.

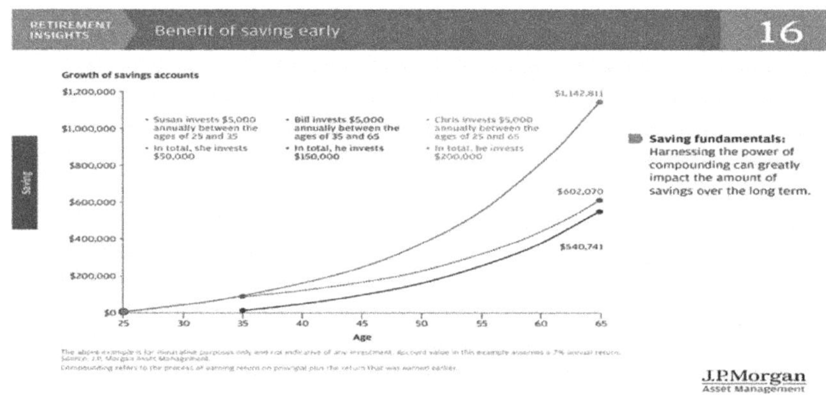

As you can see from the 3 examples here – Susan only paid $50,000 into her investment over 10 years when she was young, then let it sit until 65 where she made $602,070. Her ROI (return on investment) is 92%.

Bill started late investing at aged 35 and continued $5,000 per year until retirement at 65. His total outlay was $150,000 and his payout was $540,701. His ROI was 72%.

Chris invested $5000 every year from 25 to retirement at 65. His total spend was $200,000 and his balance at 65 was $1,142,811. His ROI was 82.5%.

So, we can see that small investments early on have the best ROI return on initial investment due to time on your side. The best monetary outcome is to start early and to pay weekly until retirement.

Chapter Five

Principles Of Wealth

My interest in life comes from setting myself huge, apparently unachievable challenges and trying to rise above them

~ Sir Richard Branson

Our money management plan is in motion and accounts will grow each day as we have utilised the concept of compounding the interest. We should feel calm that a plan will see us on track for a satisfactory retirement. Knowing me, and if you are reading this, then it will apply to you too – we don't just want a satisfactory retirement, we want the thrill of winning at investments, taking a chance on running businesses, having a stock portfolio, positive investment homes and more…

Let the fun begin!

Let's increase our learning on the Principles of Wealth, that has been foretold for many generations and can be applied in our daily lives, businesses and investments.

Your Team

Never plan to sail the ship by yourself. A team is required. Your team should consist of advisors like a solicitor or attorney, an accountant and a bank manager. An accountability partner or a coach should be there to keep you on track.

If running a business (as we all should aspire to be doing) utilise a Sales person, Marketing and digital media person, Manager of Operations, Workers and Personal assistant. Starting out can be daunting as you will not be able to afford all of these roles straight away and will find yourself wearing all the hats required. But as you get busier, taking on more work, serving more customer's needs, you will lose effectiveness unless you branch out in a team creating systems to help grow your business.

Pay Yourself First

It took me a while to really understand this one and I do see a lot of business owners and employees not taking full advantage of growing themselves too. We were brought up in a generation where we would rather be known for paying our bills on time than by growing personally richer. There is something in our makeup that says if money is light on a particular week, we should pay everyone else out first and hold our pay until we can afford it.

This is MAD THINKING.

Aren't you working? (and probably the hardest too…)

Aren't you holding all the risk?

If the risk is put to the task, doesn't it crumble like a house of cards taking you with it. Could you say that you would have benefited enough from your time spent giving all?

Who are you serving?

Ask yourself "Why are you in business/working a career in the first place?"

"Isn't your personal wealth financial status important too?"

We are primarily here in a work role or business to make money. The same can be said about personal lives. We require our finances to grow as we age. When we don't follow this principle, we remove the ability to reach our financial goals.

Isn't it important that you have a brighter future?

So, when we say Pay yourself first, you make a commitment to choose to pay yourself and your wealth funds ahead of any bills, tax obligations or any other possibility. The bills that were not paid this period can be rationalised as time progresses and will eventually be caught up, but the money you did not pay yourself has lost valuable time to compound its interest and grow. Remember, a missed $500 today in your Wealth Account for the month compounded may mean a cost of over $16,000 in 50 years in the future to your bottom line. Ouch!

Understand that Money needs to circulate
Stockpiling money under the bed (as the old saying goes) would not amount to much as the years go on if everyone did it. Money needs to circulate and enter a demand and supply cycle many times over to increase it's value. Yes, sure the bed would get lumpy and distorted with the growing piles but $5000 then would just be paper notes under a bed. But enter that same $5000 into the years of buying and selling with everybody doing it, would see that $5000 change in value. Looking back nearly 40 years ago, we can see the same houses being sold then for $26,000AUD that are today being sold for $400,000AUD. That is more than fifteen

times it's sales price in just 40 years. It is still the same house, the same land size, only minor alterations. Money in our economy has been circulating and entering deals of buying and selling that has affected the price increases by way of demand, meaning more people wanting whatever is being sold that they are willing to pay a higher price to obtain the goods. When this happens world wide, money has a chance to increase it's value over time. Now if we all stockpiled our money under our beds, where it is not entering buy and sell deals, one could assume there would be little to no change in its value, only it's amount of accumulation.

(I see a few of you are scratching your head right now…)

Money traded with another currency could increase or decrease its value depending on the supply and demand of the economy that utilises it. We see reports on the news that indicate when the value of the currencies of different countries traded for that day. The more investments that are in demand, the higher the price can be attained for it. Same as a term deposit invested with a bank, this money is not just sitting there as you see on the statement but is invested into money trades, property, businesses, etc. that will see your return being fruitful. Your money has been working.

If your money just sat under your bed, like most of the 7.5 billion people on the planet have it, it would not be a part of raising the world economy. If there were no need for supply as the demand was low, the currency value would be halted. If another country had their currencies freed up and people started buying and selling, stimulating its growth, then our currency that is not working would reduce in value. We also would need to stimulate our economy by the supply and demand cycle to see growth in value.

Back in the 1960's the average wage was approximately $4,400 per year, now in 2017, the average wage earner is meeting the equivalent of $55,387 due to inflation. Inflation is a universal calculation of the general increase in price and the fall in the purchasing value of money to determine its weighted value against other currencies.

So, don't leave money sitting in a fee-riddled bank account with no interest gained, that would be stupid like stashing it under your bed. Allow money to circulate, make it work in investments, property or safer high interest accounts.

Diversify

Have you heard the saying – "Don't put all your eggs in one

basket?" There is truth in this statement that we have to look at ways to reduce the risk and safeguard our finances. Did you know that gold bought a century ago has not really increased that much compared to business stocks or property? Funny isn't it. When we think of being rich like a King or Queen, we always invisage glittering gold. Yes, they all take their turn having spikes hitting the new highs, but also dive lower than they were before and ride the rollercoaster of repositioning. To diversify is to choose some secure safer types of investments and proportion it so the amount risked in the higher risk investments with more capacity to double your money, can be offset so as to counter a bad trade where a high-risk investment bombs out. The safer investment should be able to counteract the losses to show a make even result or close to that. As we all know, the high and medium risk investments can make substantial wins and really improve our bottom line, but also gruesome losses. It makes sense to allow for some wins but safe guard against losses.

Shake up sectors – some property, some stocks, some cash trades, some cash investment, some business entities. A fairly standard mix is 70% safe and 30% mix of medium and high-risk investing. Information is widely available on whether an investment type is classified as secure, medium or high-risk venture and is up to the investor to do their due diligence before entering into investing.

Pre-Taxed and Post Taxed Money

Most employees are being taxed by their government with post taxed dollars. That is money they receive from a job that has already had some form of tax taken out of it before it is put into your bank account. When you do your tax return at the end of a financial year, depending on what you earn, your minimal allowable deductions were bought with money that had been taxed already and you may be subjected to pay more tax.

Pre-taxed money is where a business can deduct their expenses and depreciation from their turnover (money received) before it is taxed, which depending on the ratios of income to expenses and depreciation on assets bought and the allowable deductions, it can see a tax amount being reduced. The money utilised to spend on expenses has not been taxed until the end of financial year. Meaning my $1.00 that was assessed via pre tax deductions is worth more to me than a post taxed $1.00 - tax = $0.70.

> *"I am not evading tax in any way, shape or form. Of course, I am minimising my tax. Anybody in this country who does not minimise his tax wants his head read."*
> *~ Kerry Packer*

To get the tax benefits, many wealth creators will utilise a legal entity (like a trust or company, LLC, etc) to start a business or self managed super fund so that their deductions can occur on pre-taxed dollars. There is more legal protection and more allowable deductions being in an entity for your hard-earned money compared to being an employee with post tax expenses.

Other People's Time and Other People's Money

This is probably the 2nd best wealth principle of all time – the rich do not spend their own money and risk depleting the balances of asset income to their lifestyle. They wager a deal against the funds they own to utilise other people's money for a small fee to get their next asset purchase. Therefore, they only have to worry about a small amount of interest and repayment each month rather than a chunk of asset income missing that could in turn be costlier than the face value. The asset purchased would be positive, able to produce cash flow to cover principal and interest amount, and if not, knowing it will be a temporary measure by selling or manufacturing growth on the asset to put it back into a positive status.

The way of growing bigger and faster is by expanding exponentially – for the same time, having more income streams delivering more products or services for more funds, that no cap can be put on. To do this, you cannot do it all yourself. Let me repeat this –

YOU CANNOT DO IT ALL YOURSELF. You need to trust that others can deliver at least 80% or better of what you do for a similar or better result. In this scenario, we utilise other people's time. You are the creator of your existence, if you have a good idea what is working and how to make money, then it is only natural that you will continue to work on how to generate more money and systems for others to follow. When you utilise other people's time, expanding your team, you are not only getting them to do the routine operational tasks that generate the money flow, but you also add value to the skills that you were not so good at or did not like to be involved in (i.e. sales, drafting legal documents, etc.). By utilising other people' skills and client bases, your brand can expand to levels you had not seen before, exceeding your limits of belief, year after year with no cap.

Giving

Have you heard the term 'Give and you shall receive'? This quote has a few meanings, but this wealth principle is one that you need to understand. We know money is meant to circulate. As advised before, this can create opportunities and threats, gains and losses provided that money is not stuffed in a mattress and taken out of circulation. Even the tax man gives you tax breaks to keep it circulating!

The second meaning comes from a higher power meaning that the benefits received from giving to another can outweigh the amount if generously given in the first place. Not only do you feel a sense of goodness, when we are in a higher vibration, good things begin to happen.

For example, you might get more creative and write a book, you attract a higher frequency person into your life that can show you other ways to make money, you watch another applaud your generosity and they wish to please you so much they follow your footsteps and embellish your brand as they grow themselves. It could be that others see what you did and your fan base grows due to their liking of the situation, a number of good reasons may come about from one small gesture and the follow-on moments are the bases why you continue to give.

Time Management

Understanding where your time is going each day is important in generating money. Being busy is not always an accurate picture of being productive. Are you losing time in doing operational routine tasks and not working on money producing tasks? Are you bombarded by emails that in the long term are just not that important? Procrastination is a killer – the thing we do when we feel something is hard, making us fearful or uncomfortable or plain right boring. It's best to offload these tasks immediately and work on other energising tasks that have more meaning. A simple plan can be completed in a spreadsheet looking at what is done every 30 mins over a 24-hour period for a week. There you can highlight all the tasks that were completed with a long-term view (do it once only for the progression of the business) and what was short term (repetitive tasks that you could hire someone else to do), and what was time wasting (analyse what caused this). You can also see where your flat spots are in any one day and could work on an exercise break to reconnect with body, soul and family. If procrastination keeps rearing it's ugly head, set a timer to work one task in small blocks throughout the day.

What can you *delegate, delete* or *defer*?

Always look at the next deal before entering into the forefront deal

Another golden rule is to look at the next deal before signing this deal in front of you now. What you do not want to see is the bank securing their risk by cross-securitising you or cross collateralization, which means locking all properties up in red tape so you cannot sell one property if you needed or wanted to.

The banks will always call the shots to protect their interest, not yours. Lending money for your next deal ideally should not be through the same lender as before. If the same lender is used, a good idea is to highlight the intent during this conversation before any lending contracts are signed.

Christine (my publisher) and her husband are a great example of this. They had bought their first investment property and fell into this trap. They didn't realise when they went along to the bank (one of the big four) that their loan was cross-collateralised. Which meant that although they had two loans or mortgages, they were linked together. Everything was fine until they went along to buy their third home, second investment property and applied for the loan. Everything was fine on paper in regards to servicing the loan with an 105% LVR (loan to value ratio), but as the bank wanted to cross-collateralize again it didn't fit within their guidelines. Most people would have given up at this stage, but Christine knew there must be another way.

So she increased the LVR to 80% on her two existing properties and withdrew the extra equity to use as the deposit on the third with a loan from another bank. Result!

For her fourth and fifth properties Christine and her husband remortgaged everything into separate stand alone loans so that they had more flexibility for their future investments.

Beware of too many negatively geared deals eating into your weekly wage and costing you - the time it can take to turn these investments around into a neutral or positive cash flow property or to sell can be spoilt if you find you cannot sustain these extra payments from your take home wages, a default action may occur (bank repossessing your house to cover their unpaid debt). Only the bank wins with this outcome. Recapping, if you chose to purchase a negatively geared property, make sure you have a few personal financing ways in which you can support this extra repayment, and then work on achieving a higher cash flow (increase rents, leasing space, signage, agisting, leasing rooms…) allowing this investment then being neutrally or positively geared.

Same as you think there is a good deal on the cards, and you are eager to buy into. Say a fair-conditioned block of units with good tenanted cash flow, but looking closer; the total rents are only covering the loan repayment, insurances, rates and general maintenance. The tenants are on long term contracts and rent values are locked in, but does not allow for increases until expiry of lease, if you have hit your LVR limit, there may be no more extra funds for renovations or other manufacturing of growth that would raise it's value. Ideally, we need room to move - either spare cash flow or equity in another deal that can be sourced to upgrade this deal or be available to pull against for the next deal.

Going down this path of property investing, you need to be balanced in 1. buying and selling and 2. other deals creating cash flow. Same rule is for business - Cashflow is king. Without cashflow, all movements will cease and you may be locked in contractual red tape until something shifts to aid the return of cash flow.

Plan to accumulate rather than capitalise. The properties that are being sold are the older ones that over time have been rising in value or newer ones we have added manufactured growth strategies to raise their value. The sold properties would pay down the debt of older cash flow properties. Both types of deals are as important as the other. They serve to keep you in motion to secure the next deal. Each deal should utilise the equity of the retained deals before it, limiting your exposure to risk and not deflating your wealth bottom line - your life savings.

Utilising the asset to find equity

Have you ever had an asset that cost you money every year like a block of land for example? Eventually, it will gain in value over time, but kept in the same form it will always be a negatively geared asset eating into your hard-earned money. By turning this investment into a positively geared asset, it creates cash flow and will increase in value which in turn increases your equity. (The difference between the money you owe versus the value of the investment and the loaned variable ratio LVR).

You may manufacture growth on a property by any of the following: building a house/granny flat/duplex/units etc, renovating an existing dwelling, subdividing a larger block, adding signage, sheds, new fences, etc, agisting the land, selling rocks, trees, dirt and even old floor boards from the block/house, to earn money from the asset.

I was involved in a real-life exercise where there was a block of land near the ocean. They gave us some criteria of what the location was like, the land size, the registered use, the cost to keep this block each month. We all know that to hold a vacant block of land costs unless we can create something on it or change it's material use to allow for cash flow ideas or quick flip (sell) deals.

Our task was to come up with the best use for this site. Some folk thought of a townhouse development but that was rejected as it was an industrial side of the ocean and not seen as a great area to live. Others thought of a carpark, but the council had restricted the height they wanted in this area and the extra traffic going past may affect other loading places. A hard stand development for trucks and industrial uses was suggested – a possibility but wash off residues may be a problem being so close to a natural watercourse. A combined development of food, retail, office space and rear accommodation also was brought to light. Numerous ideas were flowing and expected costs were being calculated.

But the cheapest and most rewarding idea came from the owner himself.

He did a soil test and found there was good dirt mix within. Luckily, there was a road project close by beginning and he set up a meeting. They agreed that his dirt would be able to be used in their road project and would save them delivery costs being close by. He sourced the deal. Over the duration of the project, he had created a wealthy income from the contents of that block. And you know what was the best part…?

He was now able to sell it off at a prized amount as a new marina block!

Never just think of one possibility, hone in on a few and cost it out. Look around what other people need or what an area needs to grow. Then get ideas from others that are more experienced than you. Finding partnerships or clever option deals are also ways to combat financing issues.

Remember to lower your risk and limit your exposure in the deal where possible.

Leveraging your time

To grow you must increase your income streams and we understand that you cannot be doing all of this yourself. It would be wonderful to have clones of yourself doing the same amount of sales in the one day, every day in varying locations. But that is not going to happen with just yourself. So, it is important to be able to leverage your time.

Say you were selling an online program for $300, you would not rely on selling one to one- that is one appointment, one meeting and a sell pitch and possibly one sale...or not. Let's assume this method could reach 6 clients a day over 5 work days. The maximum you could earn is up to $9000, but chances are, there will be probably one third that bought $3000. That scenario would be too time consuming when when there are so many opportunities to reach out globally by the internet channels reaching the directed target markets.

You may look at selling one to many, like presenting to a group on your hosted webinar or at a live event. By delivering valued content once to an audience, pitching the same sale once to that audience, your chances for a sale has now been multiplied. Say 150 people attended and 30% bought, would raise $13,500, and that was just an hour of your time...

Fortunately the internet and the varying audiences that interact in this space can be found live every minute of any day. Selling zero to many, can be achieved successfully by having an automated webinar via a sales funnel that works for you 24/7, adding value and pitching for sales all over the world. There is no cap on how much you can earn when putting your deal under the right audiences many times over. You only create the program once, the funnel once and drive the marketing campaign and budget as needed. However, in saying this you would have some staff to handle the marketing, correspondence, back and front-end problems and follow up on client's. Heck, you would also invest in affiliate marketers to sell your product too for a piece at the pie. "Many hands make light work", and that makes leveraging work.

Reward yourself

A fairly important drawcard is when you achieve a milestone, that there is a reward to spur this habit to keep going. If you look at putting money in a term deposit, the bank pays you dividends at the end as a drawcard to get you to do it again in the future, and you look forward to it. Same as you show up to work on a job, spend your time completing tasks to be rewarded with a pay cheque at the end of the week for services rendered. So, when you set yourself goals, there should be a reward you need to also factor in on the completion of such events. The task needs to place more dollars in your assets and the reward needs to be personal and within the realm of percent given back for the value added. This is up to you, but the idea should be kept within a percent range and not cost more than the value added to your spreadsheet.

A small reward for systemising all the operational procedures in a new business might be to take a few days holiday. The systemising is regarded as increasing the business's value and hopefully the revenue as your staff adopt the new skills. The holiday is not an expensive reward but is a marked moment of putting in tedious work hours to formulate a better run business with more upsells.

A personal goal might be to add an extra $10,000 to your yearly wage. You might take on another job or rent out a bedroom or shed. The persistence of seeing the goal achieved can be rewarded by buying a flash new outfit exposing the new driven you to meet your targets.

Utilise an entity

A safer method to protect your asset legally and having access to better tax deductions would be to utilise a tax entity. There are many forms in most countries. It is best to talk to one of your team of advisors ie an accountant and solicitor for what you want to achieve financially by the certain entity that would serve you best. Each entity has varying rules to apply during the course of business and at the time the tax year is completed and assessed. The assets operating within this entity have another layer of protection that makes it harder for another person to sue you as an individual. That means that in the eyes of the law you as the individual do not directly own the asset, but rather the entity does and you just have nominated access to control it.

In Australia, we have Companies, Trusts of varying kinds, Partnerships and Sole Traders.

In America, there are Limited Liability Companies (LLCs), S-Corporations, General Partnerships, Limited Partnerships, Sole Proprietorships and Corporations.

Chapter Six

Managing Or Operating Your Business?

I believe that being successful means having a balance of success stories across the many areas of your life. You can not truly be considered successful in your business life if your home life is in shambles.

~ Zig Ziglar

I meet a lot of business owners who are new to running their first business and have been the face of every aspect of their business in order to keep it running smoothly. Over time, they tend to hold a common belief that no-one else can do their job better. They so passionately believe this statement that it becomes their ball and chain, adding unnecessary stress which prevents them from advancing. Yes, I agree that it can be hard to ask another to take control of all the things they do, let alone work the longer hours and correctly handling the source or clients of where the revenue comes from. Plus, it can be difficult to find the right staff for hourly pay and they can be wrongly suited or under-challenged. Sometimes it can just be a trust issue that halts owners to want to seek for more help in operating their business.

A worry that another may abuse their authority given and that may have detrimental consequences to their bottom line or their position in the way the business is run. There are so many reasons that can support this statement that 'no-one else can do a better job than me', but I beg to differ.

Everything we do in operating is a learnt process. When you take over a business, you need to learn the ropes, understand your market and adapt very quickly. Staff are handpicked by you in roles you choose, which in a small business, are usually downgraded with minimal hours to save costs. But 3-5 years later, we see that the business owners that are still operating are now asking everyone "when does it get any easier?"

The answers are first and foremost, to seek advice from your team advisors, whilst also making sure your advisors are serving your needs. Secondly, you have to match and mirror a successful business in your industry. In turn, this means putting systems and procedures together that show how the business runs smoothly when you are not there. It also means developing a culture that nurtures your staff to want to add value to your business, by using rewards and engaging their skillsets. The tips and tricks of up selling, marketing to new crowds, packaging deals, partnering with other channels or suppliers, must be taught and improved upon in staffing performance guidelines. A degree of flexibility also has to be allowed.

When a feeling of family is portrayed, each staff member may feel that they contribute individually to growing your business and expressing the business's core beliefs, and building on their own talents that make this business really work. This opens up your time to set up checks within the business operations to safeguard it. The last thing you want is staff members or clients thinking you are running an open till for themselves.

With this newly exposed time, managing the opportunities and analysing the benchmarks and measures can enhance your business to grow. These include enhancing partnerships, improving relationships with your client base, promoting and marketing differently and attending seminars for new recharging ideas. Delegate any new tasks and work on your time management.

Look at duplicating and everything that we have talked about here in this book. You are the business owner. Your role is to define the direction of the business, keep an eye on all the collected data taken, add new business and be the creator of its future via innovation. The times spent operating is to define more systems and processes and check that they work properly, then train your staff to incorporate them into the business practices.

So if you had some time to start working on income producing activities, limiting your wasteful expenses, work on safeguarding your business, tinker with creating a culture, define some measures that could see how your business may grow bigger and more efficiently, work on building better relationships and so forth, wouldn't that naturally start to see a momentum that in a short time would see more money in the bank?

Business owners can afford $100 a week to pay someone 3-5 hours to handle some of the daily business tasks while they work on building the business. It is a start and it may be the baby steps to allow change in a new business owner's mindset. A lot can be achieved in small but regular intervals where focused upon. Rome was never built in a day and neither will your business be, but healthy innovative ideas and strengthening business relationships will spur your business to grow.

Some will worry that no-one will work for those meager hours, but you will see that time might be a mother's freedom to get back to a working role stepping out of the dirty nappy scene, or maybe it can be outsourced to a personal assistant who has other clients on her books as well. Maybe you already have some staff that may be looking to increase their hours and learn new roles within your business - what a great way to start cross-training your staff. As you see more revenue, you should reinvest it back into freeing up your time from operating and commit to growing your brand and your team.

When you choose to be in business, why not choose to jump fully in?

In every industry there are industry leader associations to help guide the small business's journey ahead. Usually, yearly conferences are held or training events for your participation. Associations are there for answering your questions and guiding your way to keep the industry strong. They usually offer a collective marketing campaign that works on bringing new business through your doors. Then there are supportive roles like local business networking groups, government funded workshops, mastermind groups, business advisors or coaches. All have a role to play in bettering your business and you as a business owner.

A great plus from being involved with these groups is that you get to observe how other people, similar to you, carry out their business resulting in their lifestyle. Are they tired all the time like you are? Do they struggle with money issues? Are they affected by the seasonal trends that in turn makes your leaner months leaner in your personal pay packets too? Do they have staffing headaches? Are they genuinely happy? Can they get time out to play a round of golf each week? Do they take holidays? So many questions to ask and discover what work life balance they have and can it be also possible for you too. They may have been in the game for longer, but they also started out just like you and may have some insight that may save you some pain and time along the way.

Having a business means many things to many people. Mostly, it is a significance that you can now be a key community leader, you can try your hand at something you have an interest in and you can create more money than a regular job. Some just needed to experience a more wholesome role to know that they could hold authority and be responsible for running a business.

However you think about it, I love the fact that people are out there assuming their new business roles to make a difference to their bottom line and skillsets. But the true learning comes from defining why you wanted to run your business in the first place. My reasons I first started in business was I felt dull, doing the same type of roles over and over, I wanted more for myself and a chance to make more money. I yearned for more significance, more responsibility that I had an interest in and I wanted my family to be around more, assuming roles to help out and evolve their skills in our business. Now, as I have moved on years later, learning more knowledge and looking further into myself to find what I want for creating my life by design, I feel excited by the possibilities that could be as I take each step. I consider what are my values and try to align my life with what I like and dislike, building my businesses and ultimately my personal portfolio of wealth. I am creating a brand of me that other like-minded individuals may resonate with and inspire my charted course.

In telling you this, I hope it paves the way to understand that to think you can do it all yourself by operating your business, you may actually harm the things you hold dear, restrict your abilities to grow and expand or slow your personal wealth. Operating is a stepping stone only to starting your business, 'Managing' is where the great ideas and lifestyle start to emerge.

Chapter Seven

Leverage

To bargain, take advantage of, to influence, position, gain or lift.

" The most important word in the world of money is cash flow. The most important word is leverage. "
~ Rich Dad Poor Dad

Leverage is the ability to utilise one's efforts in disproportion to the multiplying consumption or resources it takes to influence a system or environment. Taking advantage of a condition that limits costs but has extremely high gains that can be exponential.

Some of the marketing principles are to sell 1:1, 1:Many or 0:Many.

By selling 1:1, your time and one other person's time. It can be likened an individual coaching call worth $90, and therefore does not follow the definition of leverage. There is direct effort and resources put into one person but this method lacks the multiplying rewards and benefits of sales out. The maximum sale achieved is one sale, for all the time and effort expended on the sale.

If you were to increase the results by still using the same initial effort and resources, you would be utilising leverage. Seen in the 1:Many and 0:Many scenario's. You pitch your message once; like at a live seminar. Where the group of attendees in the room are visible to your pitch and message. Or you prepare for an automated video that plays 24x7, over and over to whoever is ready to watch it. Both ways offer a multiplied outcome. It is like cloning yourself to be everywhere at once, pitching your sell.

Another way you can leverage is to utilise other people's money. You put a little money out and the loan/funding handles all the risk and funds the project. The return on investment (ROI%) made can be vastly higher than if you had to source funds from your own pocket which in turn reduced your overall retirement amount.

When my son was small he grasped the concept of supply and

demand. He would come to me with his worked-out budget of how he was able to afford an item. At that time, we owned a caravan park and if there were shortages in his plan he would ask for jobs to do in the park, or ask if it was ok to sell some of his things. He had Yu-Gi-Oh cards, big collectors' items for the kids of his generation. He understood the concept of supply and demand. When the supply was short - others not having the card he had - the demand was high, allowing him to put the price up and knowing he would get a sale as it was a desirable item.

We also knew in the quiet season in the caravan park industry it was better to have rooms turned over than sit vacant collecting dust. As there was plenty of supply during the off-season, the demand for accommodation was low. So, a deal was placed for 75% of room retail price to bring in customers. Naturally, we offered extra upsells once they were staying with us in order to offset the reduced room rate. Having a lower price or a uniqueness over other accommodation providers improved the demand for our product.

The same can be seen when trading currencies, supply and demand dictates the varying price. Having some education or insight into market conditions can help take advantage of a situation and result in a multiplied effect of reward.

We are very fortunate to be in an era that instantly changed the rules of how we communicate and do business. Not only do we each have a mobile smart phone with more capabilities than just the common phone. But we also have a computer and the ability to connect with others in real time all across the world. This is huge! And the possibilities are growing every day.

Technology used to operate systems within a business have gotten smarter (and easier to use). Data collection has been automated, and there is a better understanding of why and how people are motivated to complete an activity.

No longer are we subjected to the local corner store purchase prices or limited stock options where now we can see the item we wish to purchase and pay by credit card to have it delivered in a few days. The power of selling has not only allowed products to be put under the nose of a selected niche of regular purchasers. But technology has given customers the power to compare market prices on any product across the world and in different currencies.

The establishment of buy sell sites like Amazon, eBay, Alibaba, etc, have revolutionised the way people and businesses can make money, find goods and buy via price checks. Low overheads to sell items via e-commerce sites and increased profits can be made whether you are a business or not. Remember, selling can sometimes just be a numbers game. Put your product under enough people and a certain percentage will always buy it. With the internet, your world just became the biggest targeted marketplace without a geographical or time barrier.

Everyone has a special talent or skill that is unique to them. It depends if you can apply this skill or talent with confidence that others deem valuable enough to buy. There are a lot of opportunities in the basic skillsets as many people do not have time these days to complete certain tasks required in everyday life. Basic skills can be things like cleaning, yard maintenance, tutoring children, babysitting, general administration duties, car detailing and maintenance, pet care and pet walking, for example. Some skilled services can be massage, alternative therapies, personal training, coaching, counselling, book writing, copywriting, marketing, product selling, skilled trades (electrician, plumber, block layer, mechanic, interior designer, chef, etc.).

Let's showcase an everyday person to see what she has done: *(we are looking at options to create more turnover not the costs involved in presenting)*

Case study - Jane's Cooking Classes

<u>Meet Jane:</u> Jane is a bank teller and works full time earning $38,000 per year. She struggles to make ends meet. She is a great cook and understands how different seasoning and spices work together to enhance good flavours.

To make extra money Jane was running cooking classes in her spare time at her own home. She started (1:Many) with a small group of 6 students each paying $25 generating an additional income of $150 per week

6 x $25 = $150 turnover per week.

She decided to run another class, this time in the morning of the weekend and opened it up to another group of 6 clients @ $25 each with a further $150, $300 in total.

6 x $25 = $150 x 2 = $300 turnover per week.

She soon realised she could increase her class size by changing venues (1:Many) and was able to run the same classes with 20 students @ $25 = $500.

Jane soon began to think of ways she could leverage her time and other people and had the thought "What if I had 4 events going at the same time in 4 different areas by other cooks I paid, teaching my recipes?"

By doing this she was now turning over $2000 per week. With this she looked for ways to automate this (0:Many) and teach her recipes once and have her clients pay a membership for nightly videos that could be played whilst they cook their nightly meals and they also get a downloadable shopping list.

Jane has 240 clients paying her $25 a week for her recipes, video tutorials and shopping lists resulting in a whopping $6000 income per week. Jane now wants to write a recipe book and create a 'how to' cooking program for beginners and allow recipes to be adapted to cater for the differing food intolerances and allergies presented today.

This brings over $312,000 in extra income per year and she still has the option to work a job or not.

Now that is food for thought!

What skills do you have that others want or need which could bring in an additional $100, $300 or $6,000 a week?

Chapter Eight

Venture Capital

"If you don't find a way to make money while you sleep,
you will work until you die."
~ *Warren Buffett*

Didn't life just get interesting seeing a basic idea of cooking classes turn into something quite profound? Jane is now earning more than eight times her regular yearly wage … and it does not have to stop there.

There is another explosive idea that has massive profits behind it, Venture Capital businesses. Wealthy investors are investing their capital in businesses with a view for long term returns. We all know businesses are good investment ideas, the whole taxation process is centred around giving the best outcomes to business.

It is the driving force behind circulating wealth and lifting economies.

Better rates of return on investments can come from businesses, especially a systemised and automated business with low overheads and small running costs.

Partnerships are common practice where both parties share in the risks and rewards of a joint venture. However, there is always risks in how much control versus profiting or loss can be tied up in this legal agreement. Sourcing your advisor's opinions is recommended.

Another form is Profit Sharing Agreements. Here, simply two entities coming together to share in a project, with key objectives to meet who directly and proportionately split the rewards. The two entities remain individual and only split the takings from the measurable project that has an end date attached to it.

If you have never heard the term 'white labelling' before, this is going to blow your mind.

Imagine you walked into my conference and there is a food van there selling an array of healthy food and beverages, there is a water vendor, there is a person with pens, notepads and gadgets, there is a photographer taking photos of all the attendees with high profile mentors and selling them.

Now what if I told you in this scenario, they were all my companies.

"No way… how could you afford all of that?

"And the time to run them all efficiently?"

Let me open your eyes to what rich mentors are doing everywhere. Sir Richard Branson, someone that comes to mind immediately, has approximately 400 companies with the Virgin brand. He actually only has about 30 companies he solely created and/or manages.

White labelling refers to a term where a partnership is formed between a manufacturer or supplier and 'another' (eg my conference business above). Here a product or service is produced and then rebranded by another company as their own.

So, in the conference associated businesses, no extra major contribution of capital is needed; except a legal agreement, my labels and my marketing. The products all come from individual business and I may buy them 'sale or return' for say 80% of normal retail and markup the 20% which is then my profit. Iuse my marketing brand for my benefit, while their benefit comes from increased sales and awareness.

For example the water distributor is already is a company that creates the water, they just put my label on the goods and I sell to people at my events as my own water. Same for the food van, I just have my label on the van, the merchant facilities, and selected food packaging of my logos.

The office supplies business is mine too and so is the photographer services.

Money comes into my business as 100% and I receipt them as full payment under my company brand, then pay the supplying company the 80% for services/products rendered. Within my accounting software, it would show the turnover as including the suppliers payments as 100% of the takings, even though my net profit was only 20% less associated costs. Cool right? My turnover would be $150,000, but my actual take away from this was only $30,000 less associated costs.

I don't hire people to work my white labelling businesses, but I do have a direct relationship with the already operating businesses to work and represent under my brand. They know their craft, they know how to do their business. But solely they are their own entity with all the issues businesses have. But I did not lay out much money to have them come and work under my brand. Except to open the doors to more clients I could send that way.

Just go on Amazon or eBay, look to see how the same product is marketed differently with long winded names to capture all the key words. The only difference with the product may be the label. Sellers do not always have the product sitting in their warehouse, actually they would have the suppliers at the ready so that when an order comes in, he can place an order with the supplier and have them submit his label before sending directly to the buyer. So, the seller does not have to buy loads of stock and find safe haven for them whilst he utilises time to sell it. But, he did have to trial the product well, create the label and packaging, agree to negotiate the terms to go into business together and set to work marketing his white label product. The overheads are low and his share (20%) is fair. This is called a horizontal white label business. But what if he could find another supplier that could actually manufacture the product from scratch for 40% and that would mean he could then reap 60% of the turnover. This is called a vertical market white labelling business.

Lesson here is you need other people, you need a client base and a good channel to reach the many willing buyers. Remember, it is just a numbers game of how many people you can get the attention of, that commit to a sale.

Now, I bet you are not going to sleep well tonight! All the exciting energy running around thinking up ideas on how to formulate your own empire. Sort of makes that statement – "to turn your yearly income into monthly income", seem pretty doable now.

Chapter Nine

Let's Be Humane

Contribution is a heart-centred act.

'You were born with the ability to change someone's life,
dont ever waste it.'

Giving small amounts to your heart-felt causes is catered for in the money management plan. By donating funds or time to a non-profit organisation which you care about is a wholesome endeavor to see 'good' affect the body of recipients. It also does much more than just offer help to the ones that need it. When you participate in the act of giving, good vibrations flicker through your body as you take pride in helping another. Other people can feel this and can see your physiology change. When contribution is valued and prioritised as one of the dominant human needs, the selfless act can unite people across the world in themed unison.

In Australia, our taxation system supports the donations to nominated non-profit organisations, by allowing these contributions as tax deductions.

The Law of Compensation, one of the twelve Universal Laws, states we are compensated in direct proportion to what we put forth. It is the swing in one direction that determines the swing in the opposite direction. When we give, we put it out in the universe that we are also open to receiving.

My mother, before she passed on, was the creator of a women's support group for ovarian cancer fighters. Mum was a fighter herself of a grade four cancer. Given a prognosis that women with this grade normally live two - five years, I am proud to say that she made six years. Mum was stubborn like that, she had a mother with a direct heritage of Irish and Scottish blood. There was always a fight that needed to be had on the horizon, and the mix also included that she was a redhead and a Gemini! Needless to say, that she was always frank and very direct. Mum created H.U.G.S. – Help Us Girls Survive. At this moment, I was super proud of her, raising more awareness and supporting others when her own times were grim. Looking back, this was what Mum needed to be fulfilled. She could show her gift of strength when others needed her. She could work with the best medical teams to relay new drugs of hope and hospital support. She even used her contacts to get celebrities to attend fundraising events. Mum shone!

I am surrounded by such wonderful mentors, all introducing me to their own charities and plights. There are people involved in Cambodia freeing the children from sex slavery, there are housing projects providing the basics of shelter all round the world, so is educating women in countries that do not encourage girls to attend school. There are supporters of Greenpeace trying to save our great whales and other marine life and protect our waters, and many more. But there is one special lady and her plight, and that is Lyn White of Animals Australia. My heart lies with her and her team's work, which is to maintain humane practices for animals, pushing for a kinder world.

Investigative teams are recording evidence taken from behind the closed doors of slaughter houses, piggeries, chook pens, duck ponds and farms in general. They are responsible for giving people the choice to demand better quality (i.e. eggs - free range vs cage eggs) and better practices for all farmed and wild animals. They exposed the industry in full to the public and the public demanded better care be given. For a chicken, the public demanded they be able to stretch their wings, ruffle in dirt and walk on grass. Cramped cage organisations had a major hit in 2016, where they had to finally take notice if they wanted to sell any eggs in the big chain stores. Live export has been another costly endeavour to safeguard our animals, not only on their journey in cramped trucks but also in suffocating boat hulls. They also fought for better slaughter practices, instead of the traumatic and horrific outcomes the animals have been enduring. I take my hat off to this organisation for the endless gut wrenching work they do. And I give.

The essence here is to find something that aligns with your truth and choose to help change the world for the better. It does not matter how much you spend, instead, it is about standing up, voicing your views and taking action.

We are the ones that can help to create change for the greater good for all. Having more money enables you more choice and opportunities. Your acceptance of these new responsibilities are paramount, along with your commitment to the reduction of suffering or immorality on this earth.

One great attribute of wealth educators is the need for gifting or tything. The responsibility of knowing how to build wealth successfully and the in-turn pledging contributions to focus on society's most pressing problems.

Chapter 10

Leaving A Legacy

What are you passionate about, what do you give to, or what would you like to start giving to?

"What you leave behind is not what is engraved in stone monuments, but what is woven into the lives of others."

~ Pericles

As I have watched my mother's wishes come to fruition as her Executor of her Will, I can't help but think how well she did to grow her funds after divorce. She wanted us to be proud of her, so much so that she did not take any extra funds on top of her pension as she could have.

It made me think of the importance of getting it right in the end for my line of family and loved ones.

Firstly, there has to be a place that all important documents, codes, history memorabilia and bank statements are kept.

Secondly, I think there needs to be a personal message to your loved ones, showcasing the proud moments that express just how much they belong in the family line.

Thirdly, I would like to see a plan of what you hope to achieve as the direct outcome of your estate.

"What on earth does that mean?"

Let me explain. Another mentor opened my eyes to two famous families that were able to amass great fortunes. However, only one family managed to succeed in building wealth into their dynasty years.

Imagine your grandchildren toasting to your achievements in starting your trust, which would leave them well set up in their future lives. You not only amassed some wealth, but also left behind a set of values and financial guidelines to safeguard that wealth for generations to come.

The key is that if you have created such wealth, you would like a plan to make sure the wealth remains and grows. Time is on your side with future generations, provided the benefactors understand their responsibility to protect the choices in growing that fund.

For real world examples, we would be best to look at the two most powerful families in America's past – the Cornelius Vanderbilt and John D. Rockefeller dynasties. The story of what happened to their fortunes can provide many lessons for those also planning a legacy.

The Fortune of Cornelius Vanderbilt

Cornelius Vanderbilt created his wealth in the transportation business, starting by delivering goods and passengers around New York Harbor in the early 19th century. His business grew to shipping goods from the west coast to the east coast. As the world became more mobile, his business converted from ships to trains in the railroad business, where he made the bulk of his fortune.

He died in 1877, when Vanderbilt's fortune was estimated to be $100 million, which was more than the government (US Treasury) held at the time. In today's terms, we would be talking about a fortune that was more than $200 billion.

He contributed to charities and to the Vanderbilt University, but even being the richest man in America at that time, he lived a relatively modest lifestyle. 95% of his wealth was left to his son, William Henry Vanderbilt, leaving his surviving wife and children to split the rest.

Before William's death, 9 years after his father, he could take pride in the fact that he had doubled the family fortune, but that was the last time the fortune would grow.

The Vanderbilt heirs did not follow in William's footsteps, and they later became known as wealthy socialites with a need for lavish spending.

They did not introduce new money to the trust fund, and continued the lifestyle they were famous for.

Cornelius Vanderbilt's last words were, "Keep the money together." The family fortune was all gone in a handful of generations, and just 48 years after his death, the last direct descendant died completely broke.

The Fortune of John D. Rockefeller

John D. Rockefeller grew his wealth from selling oil and kerosene in Ohio from 1870. Within ten years, his business was refining more than 90% of the oil in the United States.

Rockefeller once wrote to a partner, "We must remember we are refining oil for the poor man and he must have it cheap and good." His objective was to be dense with all levels of income earners across the population of the United States. His reputation was supported by being able to push the price of oil down from 58 cents to 8 cents a gallon.

Rockefeller died aged 97, in 1937, with more than $1.5 billion dollars. We would assume this to be estimated at over $300 billion in today's dollars.

John D Rockefeller Jr. (known as Junior), being the only son of his 5 children, was left $460 million in 1917. Rockefeller contributed more than $530 million of his fortune to charity during his lifetime.

Junior created a family trust for each of his children, where the money could be kept together. He had a group of financial professionals called the 'Family Office', managing the money which would provide Junior's kids with interest income.

The Rockefeller fortune is still being managed by the Family Office six generations later, with an estimated value of $10 billion. More than 150 Rockefeller descendants currently receive interest income from the family trusts. Following in the footsteps of John D Rockefeller, they also continue to contribute to charities.

Which family would you follow?

What was the difference between the two families in retaining and growing the fortune? It comes down to the final words of Cornelius Vanderbilt, "keep the money together." It was also the direction of the Rockefeller Family Office by protecting the fortune in a legal trust, that prohibited the erosion of taxes, lawsuits and fund depleting heirs. Not only did they have a set of values and constitution on how money could be spent, but also a portion of interest was retained in the fund that would grow its balance from year to year.

The moral of the dynasty is clear. If you want to empower your descendants, don't simply leave money for them to do as they wish. Instead, keep the money together and design a trust with a constitution of how the money can be utilised and how to keep it for future generations. The idea is to educate the benefactors on the vision that can be had for the many generations ahead of them. It does not stop with you.

Imagine your last surviving parent died and had an estate worth $2,000,000. There are 4 children, who each have 3 kids. Whilst the 4 children could have split the estate to benefit their fortunes, without financial guidelines to increase their wealth, one can assume that the fortune left to each party would diminish over time. One may also assume that the financial legacy of the original estate may not even reach the grandchildren.

Now imagine, if the $2,000,000 estate was left in a trust with a constitution of how money could be utilised and a set of values to live by. The 4 kids would be allocated supplementary incomes for the rest of their lives. They would also have an instilled set of beliefs that they did not need any handout share in the fortune, but rather a good education in wealth creation and business skills, and an opportunity to help build on to the family fortune.

Compounding interest requires time and injections of money to really work. Throughout the generations there would be time, and via the interest accumulated, there would be injections of money. The key is to balance the portions via the new generations, together with the running costs, and ensure that a portion of the interest is returned back to the fund to keep it viable.

The greatest power would come from the set of values and the wording of the constitution. The family members could be empowered to get financially educated and build a profitable business. They also would be taught life's valuable lessons of looking after health, giving to others, relationship advice and general behaviours associated with being successful. The opportunity is to get them to make good choices and this is passed on with the induction of being entitled to the trust allocation.

So, the objective is to grant them opportunities, teach them, make them strong, and also make the fund strong. To ensure that they are having a life of happiness and achievement, rather than a life of entitlement, creating "trust fund babies". With having a privileged life, there should also be role models and a strong vision that bonds their sense of belonging and care to preserve.

A financial legacy is not just about leaving money behind, it's also about educating the principles and rules for sustainable wealth and future success. Care and attention to safeguard the wealth for the next generations, idea's and thoughts, insights, a good set of values and lessons that have been learnt along the way.

In my demise, I would love to see the trust being employed to teach my successors and their families the way to build and hold wealth to benefit future generations and worthy causes.

With a sturdy constitution in place, that houses the freedom to learn how to beat the odds of dynasty failures, we will hopefully project its future survival that can affect the lives of many for generations to come.

If you haven't already done so, remember to access your bonuses with the link below:

www.portfoliomasterymeghogan.com/book-bonuses
facebook.com/groups/brainstormingbusiness

About the Author

I have a **plan, a dream, to lift people to a better personal financial status.** We **all** can achieve a better future if we start laying the foundations now.

My history is that I have always been a saver. I get more excited from **equity growth** on a balance sheet than going shopping! This is also something I am overcoming on my plan to start utilising a lifestyle fund, where fun can be had without guilt. I am not a financial advisor, but like to think I am a bit of a strategist, and also an avid learner in monetary investment practices. I have worked in banks with mainframes and ATM's, been a cash manager, worked for an electricity company and run my own businesses. And I passionately love that I have a freedom of choice, one being to fight for the ones that are mistreated inhumanely and whose voices cannot be heard.

I've had great achievements in property from building and owning our home, having investment properties, a small land subdivision and have even owned a caravan park. Believe me, there has been many mistakes on the way, but I **took action and played the game** to the best of my knowledge.

My interests lie with **what type of future I may have** and in taking steps to change the outcomes for the better.

I created this brand Portfolio Mastery, as I now see my children growing and making their life decisions, both good and bad. Friends, clients and others also seem like they could benefit from tips and tricks of financial knowledge gained, not only from learnt strategies but as a shared resource, where topics can be discussed by all willing members. I **follow** a lot of strategies from our great mentors of today; Robert & Kim Kiyosaki, Tony Robbins, Garrett Gunderson, Dymphna Boholt, Mark Rolton, Mark Anastia, Steve Essa, Scott Harris, Dean Holland, Loral Langemeier, Bob Proctor, Chris Duncan, Aaron Sansoni, Denise Duffield-Thomas, Jody Jelas, Scott Pape, to name a few. This is my portfolio of wonderful mentors that can show their mastery day in and day out.

So grateful, you came and had a look in these pages. There is something here for everyone's situation. More in depth education is seen in my Design Your Wealth Foundations e-program, as seen in the following notifications. **Let's take the time** to make changes, design fun and see growth in our plan for life.

Sign up to the Design Your Wealth Foundations e-program to get started for a small investment. Like our Facebook page Portfolio Mastery – wealth tips, ideas and opportunities, for great money tips and content. Let's begin educating ourselves on how to build more personal and business wealth for a brighter outcome.

Cheers,

Meg Hogan X

https://www.portfoliomasterymeghogan.com/shop